GOING NATIVE OR GOING NAIVE?

White Shamanism and the Neo-Noble Savage

Dagmar Wernitznig

University Press of America,® Inc.
Lanham · New York · Oxford

Copyright © 2003 by
University Press of America,® Inc.
4720 Boston Way
Lanham, Maryland 20706

PO Box 317
Oxford
OX2 9RU, UK

ISBN 0-7618-2495-2 (paperback : alk. ppr.)

To my parents

Contents

Prologue

Yet most Whites still conceive of the "real" Indian as the aborigine he once was, or as they imagine he once was, rather than he is now.
    Robert F. Berkhofer Jr., *The White Man's Indian: Images of the American Indian from Columbus to the Present*

Playing Indian is a persistent tradition in American culture, stretching from the very instant of the national big bang into an ever-expanding present and future.
    Philip J. Deloria, *Playing Indian*

The conceptual framework of this analysis is established within the reign of cultural recontextualizations. Primarily, the explanatory margin is set on Indianness as a signifier for prevailing esoteric allusions. This signifying modality, further, is dismantled in terms of esoteric iconographies of *the Indian*. For the last fifteen years, approximately, esotericism has animated and fetishized an Indian hybrid, which oscillates between noble savage and primitivism finitudes. Since the present research is an attempt to elaborate on these Indian facsimiles, divergences of authenticity or ethnic identity will be explicitly eliminated. The theoretical approach is foremost designed to be interpretive when it comes to white metaphoricality of Indian tropes, with no claim to contrastive deliberations of 'verifying true Indianness.' Accordingly, the analytical focus is on an Indian ersatz culture, which has become tremendously engulfed by New Age Indians.

A distinctive usage of terminology should prove operative in illuminating at least some complexities of auto- and heterostereotyping processes. Terms like *esoteric(ism)* and *New Age(an)* are employed as interchangeable expressions. Also, terms like *white, Caucasian, western,* and *civilized* are applied alternately. Trivialized cultural connotations, however, are denoted through discernible juxtapositions: terms like *Indian(ness), exotic(ism), primitive,* and *savage* indicate heterostereotypes, contrasting more politically correct – though still not entirely unproblematic – terms like *Native American, native,* and *indigenous.*

For the first time, New Agean hucksterism of Indianness has become vaguely identifiable in the 1980s and culminated purposefully from the 1990s onwards. The decade of the nineties and its referentiality to millennialism is a denominative period for esotericism, reeling off litanies of Indian cultures. Premillennialism – as an integrationist doctrine for apocalyptic, eschatological, and utopian theorizations alike – adhered entirely to ready-made New Agean panaceas of Indianness. Therefore, the 1990s are depicted as concise basis for disquisitions on esoteric Indianness. Also, the emblematic assortment of white shaman books discussed coheres chronologically. Contemplations beyond the year 2000/01, particularly involving post-9/11 impacts on the esoteric (Indian) industry, hence, are omitted. Notwithstanding, actual 21st century implications, especially concerning white shamanistic utilitarianism, comprise profound material for future research.

The term *white shamanism* has been selected as 'collective epithet' to designate New Agean hegemony of consummating Indianness. The appropriation of the phrase *white shaman* – originally coined by Native American writers and critics to name Caucasian poets towards the end of the 1970s, who would immodestly assume the persona of 'an Indian shaman' – should further elucidate the sphere of esoteric Indianness. While initially (and rightfully) villainized by Native American scholars, white shamanism has materialized in a peculiar way, delineating New Agean monomania of playing Indian. Slowly, but gradually, Indian imitators disjoined white shamanism from its negative inferences, reversed it, and, above all, made it become infatuated with esoteric hodgepodge. Today, white shamanism encapsulates a multitude of esoteric Indian orations.

New Agean counterfeit Indians have mobilized a certain form of 'global tribalism.' White monopolies of going Indian, still, have predominance in the United States. However, globalization offers all-compelling platitudes for white shamanism. White shamanic trespassing on the 'Indian Land of Enchantment' motivates cultural possessiveness. Its merits transcend the mere commercial marrow to subjugate Indianness as a means of cultural "pop hedonism"[1] for customers in the western hemisphere. Moreover, white shamanism relishes an Indian microcosm of 'tribal clones.' Cloning (Indian) tribes, again, is embossed with a certain explicitness of 'Anything goes.'[2] Impersonating 'true' Indianness – for white shamans – has become severed from actual time and place. In fact, it is honed as virtual Indian reality. This 'cybernetic Indianness,' then, encompasses all-white, revisionary affectations. Since white shamanism, once and foremost, conflates 'synthetic' Indian cultures with blunt Caucasian itineraries, it exceeds traditionally white masquerades or imitations of Indianness like Indian Hobbyism, for example. Indianness white shaman style is rather 'internalized' through mythmaking mechanisms.

Consequently, white shamanism avails itself of Indian cultures for thorough introspection, with Indianness being primarily 'mentalized.' Indian individuation – hence the attribute 'white' with shamanism – is no longer a matter of birth, heritage, or upbringing, but a conscious choice that anyone, according to white shaman teachings, can successfully make: going Indian in mind/spirit, or via the esoteric hypothesis of reincarnation, is their primordial denomination. White shamans' 'spiritual' Indianness, by and large, is symbolically underpinned by new modulations of primitivism. Primitivist monumentalism, transpiring since the late 1960s, has caused expressive alterations of noble savage images. The increasing physical-erotic liberalization within western societies has resulted in a steady disembodiment/desexualization of so-called noble primitives. Once exoticisms of bodies, due to sociopolitical and psychohistorical reasons, started to saturate at the beginning of the 1990s, noble savage cliches had to be reinvented. Parallel to whites going mentally/spiritually native, primitive people went *neo*-noble. At times when spiritual healing of hypercivilized citizens turned into the bottom line for numerous New Age movements, the appropriation of neo-noble savages boomed. Inevitably, primitive wisdom, prophecies, visions, and meditations submitted an almost endless repertoire for truth searching esoterics – and white shamans. What they are after is no longer the noble savages' physiognomic aesthetics as antidote to civilization's discontents. Their interest is explicitly directed towards the primitive mind as escapist totality for a supposedly jeopardized white existence. This apotheosis of the neo-noble mind, however, always remains within boundaries of postcoloniality by maintaining differentiations of (white) intellect and (savage) instincts.

Superimposed onto white shamanism, this monolithism of civilized ratio versus primitive emotio concentrates particularly on the neo-noble Indian figure. White shamans and their disciples mentalize and, again, mystify and marginalize stereotypical ideas about the Indian. Labeled neo-noble, Indians are valorized and homogenized as omniscient concerning everything metaphysical and precivilized. Ill defined like that, neo-noble Indianness suggests more than simply another form of "a passionate commitment to inverting Christian-Humanist values, out of a conviction that the Indian's way of life is preferable."[3] It does not merely discourage polyphony and postmodernity of Native American cultures, but also proposes to eclipse visibility and versatility of these cultures alltogether. By exhibiting and retailing a synthetic Indianness without exasperating reprehensions to the mainstream public, white shamanism authorizes itself to take over custody of Indian culture. The side effects of this white shamanic neo-imperialism are substantially chiasmic: going native makes natives *re*vanish.

Notes

1. Daniel Bell, *The Cultural Contradictions of Capitalism* (New York: Basic Books Publishers, 1978), 72-76.

2. The 'Anything Goes' attitude of today's esoterics is a by-product of pop hedonistic paradigms, originally building in the fifties. Astrology, especially, galvanized post-World War II textualities of esotericism. Palpable antagonisms of narcissism and anxiety, as, for instance, discussed in Adorno's *The Stars Down to Earth* in terms of astrological patterns, also emphasize the nineties' tradition of New Agean happiness/balance. Cf. Theodor W. Adorno, "The Stars Down to Earth, " in *Gesammelte Schriften: Soziologische Schriften II*, ed. Rolf Tiedemann (Frankfurt am Main: Suhrkamp, 1997), 9/2: 7-120.

3. Leslie A. Fiedler, *The Return of the Vanishing American* (New York: Stein and Day Publishers, 1968), 169.

Acknowledgments

My most sincere expression of gratitude to those who have provided – and continue to provide – help through patience, understanding, and emotional encouragement. Grateful appreciation also for financial support and technical assistance.

Introduction

The European image of the Indian oscillated between the noble savage and
the bloodthirsty devil.
   Brian W. Dippie, *The Vanishing American: White Attitudes and U.S.
Indian Policy*

We speak in terms of primitive and advanced, almost as if human minds
themselves differed in their structure like machines of an earlier and later
design.
   Jack Goody, *The Domestication of the Savage Mind*

Any discussion of 'the going native recipe' would be incomplete
without analyses of its two main 'ingredients': (ig)noble savage images
and primitivist ideologies. Therefore, the succeeding discourse is
aimed at outlining the (ig)noble savage/primitivism dyad as
explanatory matrix for the 1990s' phenomenon of going native. First of
all, a historic sketch of the mythogenesis of (ig)noble savage as well as
primitivist impressions should prove auxiliary for demonstrating and
comprehending contemporary developments of this phenomenon. Over
centuries, compartimentalizing the savage-construct in either
demonized or victimized figures has gained paramount subtlety, most
prevalent, for example, in movies like *Dances with Wolves*.

This trajectory of noble/ignoble dichotomies represents a prelusive compendium for white shaman maladaptations of Indianness, which, then, are further particularized by primitivist neologisms. Thus, the final part of this introduction incorporates a close-up of the maturation of neo-primitivism. Analogously, the passim tapestry of the prefix *neo* is investigated as a crucial entity to construe a substantial shift within the axis of body-mind affinities.

The Mythogenos of the Neo-Noble Indian

The concept of the 'savage' is almost always established as a mirror image to the 'civilized citizen.' Depending on the momentary perception of civilization by the civilized, savages are defined either by what they lack or what they represent. A retrospective evaluation of (Euro-American) history shows that savages always turned ignoble whenever the dominating (Euro-American) culture needed proof of being civilized. This rationale changed rapidly as soon as civilization was considered to be degenerated, which led inevitably to the formation of the noble savage picture. The dichotomy resulting from this interrelation is anything but realistic. Both portrayals – the ignoble as well as the noble one – are doomed to be and to remain extremely pattered and abstract. It is a set-up of contrasts that hardly corresponds with actual life, for it is determined by a decidedly black-and-white structure. Features, character traits, and habits become classified through the polar terms *good* or *bad* and unilaterally applied to the noble or the ignoble savage image. As these two images are unequivocally defined by positive or negative aspects, they can never turn out to be holograms. Instead, these portrayals stay flat and particularly one-dimensional. There is no differentiation except for blatant good or bad. Individual portrayals with intermingling positive and negative features are nonexistent. The only aspect that counts is the collective with any gray areas missing. Thus, both concepts – the ignoble *and* the noble – resemble stereotypes, reenforcing prejudices rather than deconstructing them.[1]

Initial conceptions of the savage derivative have already been etymologically adjacent to habitat by implementing the term savage as "a variant of the Latin *silvaticus*, meaning a forest inhabitant or man of the woods."[2] The savage assuming the role of nature's/wilderness' inhabitant is an interesting image, which needs to be analyzed beyond etymological reconceptualizations. Both roles, the savage as child (i.e., noble) or beast (i.e., ignoble) of the woods, are crucial in understanding civilized society's perception of this image. By representing a territory, which is distinctively separate from the civilized world (i.e., the city), the savage environment typifies everything the urban one is not. Whenever the city is seen as the stronghold for technology and progress, the savage world turns into a dangerous, enigmatic wilderness, which is meant to be subdued and conquered. At times when urban life is perceived as too overbearing by the majority of its inhabitants, this wilderness, then, connotes freedom. The clear-cut distinction between 'natural' and 'artificial' world becomes a convenient model for dystopian and utopian visions alike. This dichotomy of dystopia and utopia, bound to a definite opposition between savagism and civilization, is another crucial source for the reproduction of stereotypes.[3]

Ethnocentric as well as ethnostalgic stereotyping has always been an integral part of how civilized society perceives and patronizes savages. Fascination and dismay with savagism is a common theme at any time and place in history, whether it is Tacitus' *Germania* or Columbus' travel reports, for example. The prototypical noble savage, commonly associated with Romantic Naturalism, originated far beyond the 19th century. Moreover, the so-called child of nature was colorfully depicted in antiquity. This innocent and virtuous creature of the Golden Age was the classical counterpart to the ignoble, promiscuous savage.

With the discovery of the New World, it was a mere consequence that traditional European attention to the noble-ignoble dichotomy should be immediately engrossed by savage inhabitants of this continent. Henceforth, Native Americans became the new medium for old stereotypes. Columbus, for instance, praised their generosity and physical aesthetics, the implications being that these savages could never amount to anything else but (mute) servants.[4] The explicit denial of savage intelligence, involving more than just 'common sense' and 'natural instincts,' is particularly noticeable, for it prevents any equality between savages and Europeans in the first place. Columbus' remark about 'his' savages being gentle natured and, thus, would make perfect slaves is exemplary in that it epitomizes the general mood of Europeans classifying any newly discovered tribe as either *friend* or *foe*: friends, hospitable to the European newcomers, would personify the ideal targets for Christianization and civilization – the aim, however, never being their status of equality (measured by European standards). Rather, they should be missionized in the sense of becoming 'tamed,' so that they would make ideal (i.e., harmless) labor forces.[5] Those being war-like and unpredictable, represented the beast-like savages. The emphasis on animalistic features of this group made it easier for Europeans to believe in and justify the extinction of these savages. As they posed a threat to the spreading of civilization, they became degraded to an inhuman status and, thus, legitimized to get killed.[6] – In Scott B. Vickers' words: "The Ignoble Savage clears the way for colonial expansion, conversion, and extermination. The Noble Savage clears the way for assimilation, appropriation, and spiritual poverty."[7]

A closer look at particular aspects of noble and ignoble images is essential for understanding the mythogenesis of the Indian.[8] This Indian figure is predominantly characterized by stasis and homogeneity. Both images – the ignoble as well as the noble – are explicitly static, meaning that stereotypical Indians are being denied any evolutionary development whatsoever. Therefore, these images are exclusively historic ones, placing Indians in pre-Columbian times and surroundings, which are either idyllic or barbarian, according to noble or ignoble attributes. Indians and, moreover, all Indians categorically are doomed to experience no (mental, physical, emotional) evolution beyond that point in history. This homogenous picture of the so-called Indian Nation leaves no room for differentiating between the various tribes and their individual tribal structure, life, and culture.[9] The preference for the Indian collective rather than Native American individuality is another means to stereotype and turn this ethnic group into a faceless mass. The opacity of this mass, then, is a vindication for positive and negative generalizations of any kind. The visual image is particularly afflicted by this technique of generalization. The prototypical Indian has long, dark hair, a hooked nose, and coppery skin,[10] wearing traditional Indian 'costumes'[11] and jewelry. Particularly when it comes to Indian outfits, the inchoate picture of pre-Columbian times strikes again. It is George-Catlin- and Edward-Curtis-apparels with eye-catching feathers and peace pipes. The painter George Catlin and the photographer Edward Curtis, both trying to capture impressions of the vanishing race in the 19th century, are made responsible for having created some of the most persistent stereotypical images of Indians. George Catlin's Indians are depicted through the scheme of noble-ignoble savage, sometimes picturesque, sometimes committing the most despicable atrocities.[12] Sanitized Wild West images are especially propagated through Edward Curtis' patterned visual portrayals of, for example, the Indian 'chief.' Besides, since Curtis never cared very much for authenticity, he merely used his Indian objects to pose with ready-made 'trinkets':

> Curtis provided a limited inventory of "Indian" props such as feather bonnets, masks, and costumes, which frequently resurfaced haphazardly in his photographs of members of different tribes. In later photographs he used wigs to disguise the short hair worn by many of his Indian subjects and cropped and retouched prints to remove all signs of White contact, thereby enhancing homogenized and allochronic notions of "Indianness."[13]

Contemporary perceptions of 'real' Indian gowns, still, are dominated by a motley mixture of several tribal entities, deriving from the most famous tribes like, for instance, Sioux or Apache. The Sioux feather bonnet – along with Apache headbands and 'typically Indian' jewelry like squash blossom necklaces or turquoise bracelets – is by far the most favored Indian 'trinket.' As John C. Ewers puts it: "Among whites the mistaken idea was implanted that an Indian who does not wear a feather bonnet is not a real Indian of importance."[14] The George Catlin and Edward Curtis images, however, contain two other aspects that influence contemporary images of Indians: *stoicism* and *the vanishing race*.

The stoic Indian, never showing any emotional reaction, is a very complex stereotype, involving more than just facial expressions. Since most of Curtis' photographs have been taken of Indians previously expelled from their homelands, they look grave and serious. This image of the stone-faced Indian has stuck in white brains ever since. Several Native American writers, for instance, Vine Deloria Jr. and Gerald Vizenor, have attempted to work out humor and the picaresque as significant aspects of Native American tribal cultures and history. But also non-native authors have commented on this fact. Louise K. Barnett, for example, interconnects Indian stoicism with another cliche – Indian torture: "According to the general stereotype of the Indian, the stoical endurance of suffering and death is a valued quality."[15]

The stoic Indian posture, further, is exceeded by pathetic gestures and simplistic talk, the so-called Tonto language. Tonto, the dumb appendage of and counterpart to the Lone Ranger, became exemplary for the mute TV Indian, uttering verbal bits and pieces. Tonto's language and particularly his position in the plot epitomize the stereotype of the taciturn, naive savage:

One Indian caricature, however, continued to vie with Blacks for top honors by white entertainment standards. That was Tonto, the "friendly Indian companion" of the Lone Ranger. "Kemo sabe" and "get-em up Scout" showed white people that Tonto knew his linguistic place. Tonto, with his clipped baby talk had at least advanced the Indian from "ugh" to "kemo sabe." But the Lone Ranger's vocabulary and mellow Waspy voice befitted the white half of the act. Whatever the Lone Ranger was, Tonto was less – less fast, less a sharpshooter, less domineering. Even his horse, Scout, was less white.[16]

If the Indian is allowed to talk at all, it is always in a certain form of metaphoric language. Typical Indian expressions are supposed to include references to 'Mother Earth.' The Indian as keeper of the earth, living in harmony with 'Mother Nature,' is another cliche, establishing them as first, 'true' environmentalists. This cliche, again, links up with the vanishing race matter. Indians have always been associated with nature, counterpoising progress and technology. They stand for loincloth-bearer-aptitudes. As there is practically no 'untouched' nature any longer – with even the most remote parts of wilderness like the Arctic and Antarctic contaminated by pollution – stereotypical Indians, existing in a balanced symbiosis with their environment, cannot help but fade.

Their place in society, thus, is an invisible one. If anything, they become relics of the past and museum specimens, scrutinized under civilization's microscope like fossils. Society's expectations also provide them with traditional occupations of handicraft and artwork. An Indian pursuing anything else but weaving, pottery, or bead making is a curio. A 'literate' Indian, holding down a 'sophisticated' job, is still met with surprise. Careers in the academic/economic world and financial success on the job market seem to be a paradox to their Indian 'heritage' of sitting in front of a tepee or campfire, being wrapped in a blanket, and chanting war whoops. They are considered to remain exhibits of the past instead of taking part in the present or even the future. The image of the retrograde Indian is a very recalcitrant one and, thus, contributes most to the sober picture of Indian existence.

This unrealistic perception results in explicit black-and-white patterns, giving rise to either noble or ignoble Indians. The noble Indians are altruistic and characterized by an innocuous and infantile naivety. It is particularly these elements of sharing – as, for instance, implied by the Thanksgiving Saga – and child-like innocence that make noble Indians a target for white pity. These Indians embody passive victims, crushed by civilization's greed. The ignoble Indians, contrastingly, are a blight to civilization. Their fierce looks and customs, their sexual prowess, and their laziness represent hazards to civilized life. Total ignorance of civilization's concept of sin or crime makes them live beyond conversion. By being inclined towards torturing and by lacking mental capacities that would go beyond animalistic instincts, they pose a certain libidinal threat to civilization. Earliest, most subtle literary depictions of this threat can be found in captivity narratives, for example.

As being a predominantly media-influenced one, the protean Indian image manifests itself especially in Hollywood's movie picture industry. Hollywood's proposition of what an Indian should look and behave like in a movie mirrors the pro tem public opinion of the savage picture. This Indian chimera either yields to noble or ignoble characteristics, according to the contemporary public taste. The glorious western movie of the John Wayne era, for instance, displayed 'Indianized' Europeans in long-hair wigs, facial paint, and typified garments. Their position in the plot was a marginal and menial one, personifying the typical villain.[17] The General Sheridan model of the only good Indian being a dead one was unswerving in these movies: the white hero would not squander with Indians, but kill them off instead. As attitudes towards 'the Indian cause' changed in the 1960s and 1970s, so did Hollywood's portrayal of Indian figures. Most of the times, Indian movies of the sixties and seventies became a vehicle for expressing political circumstances: "The Indian movies made then, such as *Little Big Man* and *Soldier Blue* (both 1970), films that indicted the American Army for practicing genocide on the Native American, were partly the expressions of the producers' and directors' feelings about Vietnam."[18] This social metacontext also manifested itself in Hollywood's public attitude. Marlon Brando, for example, considered it a politically and socially critical action of boycotting the Academy Awards Ceremonies in 1973, having a certain Sacheen Little Feather (who afterwards got to be known as Marie Louise Cruz) in a 'traditional Apache costume' receive his Oscar.

Unalloyed black-and-white paradigms, readily applied in earlier films, tumbled down and got replaced by a more prevaricate presentation of Indian-white constellations. Again, the pliable Indian image was rather controlled by white sympathy, pity, and guilt than an unadorned attempt to show realistic facts. Hollywood's pro-Indian movie production reached its peak at the beginning of the 1990s. Kevin Costner's *Dances with Wolves* (1990) triggered a flood of films dealing with the Indian as noble savage, most of the times brutalized by white

expansion and greed. *Dances* paved the way for Hollywood
blockbusters like *Last of the Mohicans* (1993), for Disney films like
Squanto (1994), *Pocahontas*, and *The Indian in the Cupboard* (both
1995), and semidocumentaries like *Lakota Woman* (1994). The almost
endless list continues with *Legends of the Fall* (1994; though not on an
Indian topic, still, appropriating Indianness), *Hawkeye* (1994), and *The
Broken Chain* (1994). A good example of a film less successful with
the audience, due to "a stark, realistic view of Hurons and missionaries
in the 17th century, . . . the less attractive actors, violence, and
unpleasant story line"[19] is *Black Robe* (1991). All those movies and TV
shows in unison have a new flavor added to the well known noble
savage picture: the disclosure of Indian spirituality/shamanism, inner
balance, and environmental harmony.

These prestigious features correspond exactly with general market
trends, discovering the Indian as esoteric bestseller. The congruence
between both the movie industry, sequestering Indian nobility, and
white shamanism, unfolding at the dawn of the 1990s, is no mere
coincidence. The receding 1980s and approaching 1990s demarcated a
new era for spin-offs of esoteric Indian criteria. Parallel to becoming
absorbed by esotericism, Indianness was also infused with pervasive
shamanism. This three-part scheme (i.e., Indianness-esotericism-
shamanism), then, entailed relevatory vicissitudes. Kevin Costner's
Dances with Wolves, for instance, connotes particularly glib variations
on cultural colonization. As frequently argued, Lieutenant Dunbar's
character is implicitly posed to essentialize one of the first New Agean
shamans on the (movie) screen. His hermit's life at Ford Sedgewick
enunciates the 'special and powerful medicine,' acknowledged by the
Indians he later comes to live with. Thus, the metasemiotics of *Dances*
can be read as the threshold for the 1990s' white shamanism.
Abandoning civilization and all its deeds for a virgin land frontier,
Dunbar's character goes native by finally being diametrically opposed
to Indians and non-Indians alike: towards the end of the movie, a third
space is disclosed by Dunbar's and Christine's Indianness. They are
'Indianized' enough to surpass their Caucasian fellows in wisdom,
spirituality, and environmental harmony, yet – unlike their 'Indian
soulmates' – still 'whitenized' to an extend that guarantees exemption
from ethnic harassment. For this purpose, *Dances* amalgamates
(ig)noble features with postcoloniality.

At best, genuine Native Americans perceive this development with
wry humor, and an increasing number of Native American academics
and writers resorts to deconstruct the most blatant aspects of this movie

picture. While assuming *Dances with Wolves* as a definite caesura in the movie business, whence audience and producers got more sensible towards Indianness, these authors, still, show how untenable movie policies basically are. In particular, they focus on unsubstantiated aspects, that perpetuate white patronization and benevolence in order to discredit Indian film parts. *Dances*, by far, exemplifies the most prominent of these aspects. The protagonist, for example, is always white and, above all, purely white – never a 'half-' or even 'full-blood.' One of Hollywood's biggest taboos, a protagonist couple of mixed ethnic descent, is very much inherent to Indian movies of the 1990s as well: the female counterpart to this hero (naturally, every 'true' protagonist is a man) is also white and – as shown by Christine in *Dances* – a character to introduce possible captivity elements. The 'real' Indians, though compared to former films at least portrayed as characters and not so much as plain, extra-like figures in the plot, are still endowed with certain well-known qualities. For instance, they are indigent, but happy and, as they represent the noble savages, audacious and hospitable. These noble savages, however, always coexist with ignoble ones. The typical 'goody' Indians most often derive from popular tribes, like the Lakota Sioux, for example. The 'baddy' Indians are set apart from this image in a distinct visual way by lacking famous Indian paraphernalia or hairstyles. Their chief won't wear a headbonnet or pathetically carry a peace pipe, but a tomahawk instead. They would not be traditional 'longhair' but have shaved heads. 'Baddy' Indians usually personify scouts for white parties. Therefore, their missing long hair is meant to indicate their abandoning of 'old (Indian) ways.' By embracing white ways, they are coded traitors to their heritage. In addition to that, they would usually appear with (red) war paint on their faces and, thus, personify the typically abysmal Red Skin. This 'goody-baddy' constellation is accentuated to win and ensure the audience's emotional reaction. The strategy of dignifying one group while condemning the other allows the expression of two basically contradictory strands: an accusatory tone when dealing with white policies plus the justification of these policies in certain situations. Robert Baird explains this strategy as follows:

Another strategy for resolving the historical trauma and contradiction of The Massacre is, through sleight of hand, to present viewers a tribe of "Noble Savages" (The Sioux in *Dances* and the Cheyenne in *Little Big Man*), and then a tribe of just plain old fashioned savages (the Pawnee in both films). This strategy has the function of addressing white historical fear and guilt within the same narrative, providing a way in which a fiction can remain simultaneously true to contradictory emotional responses to history.[20]

This 'goddy-baddy' antithesis, naturally, is also projected onto white characters. As shown in *Dances*, some white characters are especially designed to bring in aspects of overcivilization like, for instance, insanity in the case of Major Fambrough. Parallel to 'good' whites, some of whom might be dispassionate, but still tolerant to Indians, while others, again, would even assimilate to Indian ways and play Indian, there is always the group of hard-headed Indian haters. They are the ones – and the ones only – who are disingenuous, killing off Indians irrespectively. After all the 'genuine' Indians get dislocated and/or exterminated, it is up to their white 'blood brothers' to carry on 'their ways.' This twist of 'true' Indians being banished from the screen at the end of the movie, whereas white, assimilated Indians remain, is a crucial device for leaving the audience complacent. The acerbity, lurking in the Indians' indeterminate, tragic lot, is neutralized by auspicious white characters, still playing Indian. As any movie can only be successful by emotionally touching but not shocking people, this ending is the most adequate solution. Indian exile and disappearance is not to be considered distressing as long as there is whites inheriting their ways:

> But as the films unfold, the categories of "Indian" and "white" get blurred in surprising ways. Both these films include white men and women who are coded "Indian," either by adoption and long acculturation, or else by their instinctive sympathies. These whites share the Native Americans' strong, empathetic response to nature. What's more, and very important, the whites are allowed to stand at the movie's end as the inheritors and perpetuators of Indian ways after the actual Indians are dead or as good as dead. The result is curious: the films initially define Indians as different from whites, but then show how the best among the whites think and feel like Indians. Bad white people usurp the Indians' physical space; but good whites move into their mental and spiritual space. And once whites occupy the space close to nature that has been coded as "Indian," actual Indians have nowhere to go but off into the proverbial sunset.[21]

A New Era of Primitivism

Primitivism is neither an endemic phenomenon, nor is it restricted to any specific time in history. Considering mankind's development from a sociohistorical perspective, primitivist as well as antiprimitivist periods are reoccurring. Due to the antagonistic relation between 'progressive' civilization and 'regressive' savagism, every cultural group experienced and experiences periodic waves of primitivism. Such primitivist heydays are predominantly bound to cultural leaps in technology or science, for example. Whenever culture and cultural achievements become too oppressive or artificial, human psyche – whether consciously or unconsciously – utilizes escapist techniques. Such escapist modes usually incorporate primitivist characteristics. For instance, feelings of alienation from overcivilized society are overcome by resorting to typically primitivist simulacra of the tribal collective. This process of thought, of course, can also be reversed whenever the individual's personal constraints result from society's rules and regulations. Primitive communities, then, appear as vital ground for individuality and privacy. Furthermore, as the cultural construct is experienced as something overly suffocating, the liberating aspect of savagism is particularly emphasized. The perceived entropic state of technology with its prolific number of stimulants is set into contrast by an idealized simplicity and sobriety of the savage existence. Savage life is depicted as uncorrupted, even naive, with no negative pitfalls whatsoever. Amplification of both negative aspects of civilization and positive aspects of savagism is a standard procedure, even in normally clandestine primitivist thought.

In most cases, primitivism is either linked to certain topographical or temporal settings. Topographically, it is necessary to distinguish actual/realistic (i.e., the jungle or tropical islands) and fictional/mythical (i.e., Arcadia, Atlantis, Eden, Elysium, Tirnanogue, Xanadu) sceneries.[22] Temporal settings, for instance, would involve certain (pre)historic stages of mankind. In earlier discussions about primitivism, prehistory has been explicitly excluded. However, an evaluation of contemporary primitivist tendencies needs to focus on certain elements of prehistoric societies as well. Prehistory, generally, is defined as a time prior to mankind's ability to read and write. Literacy, then, has developed into a cultural connotation with several aspects such as rationality, for example, attached to it. Since postmodern society's discontent is partly due to the perceived overemphasis of logic reasoning and scientific knowledge, neo-primitivist tendencies always include particularly common notions of illiteracy and prehistory in terms of instincts, suspicion, and common sense.

With reference to Freud's *Civilization and Its Discontents*, Arthur O. Lovejoy and George Boas have classified this specific type of primitivism 'cultural' (versus 'chronological'), calling it "the discontent of the civilized with civilization, or with some conspicuous and characteristic feature of it."[23] Primitivism and primitivist sources – both cultural as well as chronological – date back to Greek and Roman times. *Primitivism and Related Ideas in Antiquity* is a profound study, demonstrating some of the most primal concepts and perceptions, which Europe's earliest cultures have applied to their 'barbarous' neighbors. It is an intrinsic synopsis of coherent philosophical and political ideas about the savage Other. Thereby, Lovejoy and Boas have stressed the persevering character of primitivist theories. Tracing the history of primitivist ideas or complex of ideas – in the vocabulary of Arthur O. Lovejoy – merely to Jean-Jacques Rousseau is a rather myopic endeavor. Primitivist tendencies also survived during the Middle Ages, though their tradition was never as evident as in classical antiquity or the Renaissance. The prototype of the medieval savage was the Wild Man. Due to the strong influence of Christian dogmas at that time, primitivist descriptions were also colored by biblical connotations. Additionally, nature had to be embedded in a Christian context, otherwise it represented a potential danger of blasphemy: "The danger to Christian orthodoxy in the appeal to Nature was the possible disregarding of God. It must therefore be proved either that the Law of Nature was the Law of God or that the appeal to Nature was illegitimate."[24] Moreover, primitivist formulas exist throughout history, paralleling mankind's constant shift in between the polarities of nature and culture. Accordingly, primitivist ideas get revived or denigrated at any time. Besides, any primitivist context is superimposed by a hierarchical structure, meaning that a particular cultural or ethnic group of people considered barbarian by other cultures, again, directs their own primitivist perception onto another group.

The general anachronism of positive and negative components being united in the savage image derives from distinct historical traditions. Classical thought, on the one hand, emphasizes an overwhelmingly idyllic state of simplicity and integrity, whereas the Judeo-Christian view, on the other hand, has its focus on bestial or devilish interpretations of primitivism. The Renaissance savage figure is generally assumed to have been modeled after ideas from antiquity exclusively. A closer look, however, reveals a quite pragmatic mixture of both classical as well as Judeo-Christian characteristics. Additionally, the discovery of the New World brought forth a flood of strange impressions for Europe. With travel reports about alien territories and their exotic inhabitants, fauna, and flora, primitivism also became an economic factor. For Christopher B. Steiner, the Age of Discovery is pre-eminent for manifesting Europe's idea about the exotic Other:

> Primitives in the Age of Discovery appeared to be identical throughout the globe because, wherever they were encountered, they were portrayed and represented by the same people – European observers who reduced them to a metaphor of Otherness that served only to confirm European expectations of the exotic rather than to challenge those assumptions.[25]

Popularity of the idealistic primitive life (contrasting European civilization) prevailed, despite such differentiating statements of, for example, Thomas Hobbes, for whom the absence of institutional law and order in any nature-affiliated environment equaled evil. Michel de Montaigne's writing, though often oversimplified as idealization of nature and primitivism, displays a by far greater contextual significance. His analysis of the nature-culture dichotomy is closer to being didactic than sentimental, characterized by a critical evaluation of the benefits and ills of primitive and civilized life alike. While being credited for coining prototypical primitivist phrases, Montaigne never explicitly describes the resort to nature as panacea or means of escapism. His influence is considered to be most evident in William Shakespeare's portrayal of Caliban. In *The Tempest*, Shakespeare questions – some critics would even go as far as to use the term 'mock' – primitivist enthusiasm. The play harks back to primitivist as well as progressivist ideas and, thus, appears as "a comedy in praise neither of nature nor of civilization, but of a proper balance between them."[26] Montaigne's essay *Of Cannibals* and its interpretations triggered a profound discussion about (human) nature. Conceptions of the savage mind, as set in opposition to civilized artificiality, even manifested themselves in empiricist models of thought by scholars like John Locke and David Hume.

Jean-Jacques Rousseau, still, is to be seen as the founding father of the noble savage par excellence. As with the case of Montaigne, his writing has been made into an epitome of ideas and images associated with the noble savage and environmentalism. His *Discourse upon the*

Origin and Foundation of the Inequality among Mankind has become reduced to standardized keynotes such as 'the virtues of nature' or 'the child of nature,' when, indeed, Rousseau assumed a somewhat relativistic bias towards primitivism. Primitivism has always been a literary device to demonstrate political and/or philosophical interpretations of civilized society's malaise. The Enlightenment adapted primitivist ideas for educational purposes. Reformist statements about the ills of civilization got peppered with references to primitive cultures as a plain stylistic means. In fact, no writer constructed these analogies to make citizens actually appropriate savage ways of living. Philosophers of the Enlightenment did by no means unquestioningly embrace the noble savage model. They were very well aware of the danger of sentimentalizing the savage figure, just like they knew about their elitist position as educated literati, writing for a comparatively small and equally educated audience. The overwhelming part of society that was meant to be altered did not have access to those theories anyway – the actual status of the 'common folks' almost equaling the enlightened philosophers' perception of the savage. Benjamin Keen summarizes this typical Enlightenment view as follows:

> Most *philosophes* conceded that the savage possessed certain virtues, but they were aware of the material and cultural poverty associated with his condition. A typical Enlightenment view described the savage state as the childhood of the race. The savage might display an admirable simplicity, candor, courage, and nobility of spirit, but he was prey to deplorable passions, and his lack of control over his environment exposed him to terrible miseries and privations.[27]

The emphasis on primitivist rationality during Enlightenment, naturally, got altered to emotionality in the Romantic Age. Romanticism dissected primitive life and its symbolic power in terms of sensibility and sentimentalism, which – in the Romantic opinion – should enhance the lackadaisical sobriety of civilization or, as Roderick Nash describes the *Romantic Wilderness*:

> "Romanticism" resists definition, but in general it implies an enthusiasm for the strange, remote, solitary, and mysterious. Consequently in regard to nature Romantics preferred the wild. Rejecting the meticulously ordered gardens at Versailles, so attractive to the Enlightenment mind, they turned to the unkempt forest. Wilderness appealed to those bored or disgusted with man and his works. It not only offered an escape from

society but also was an ideal stage for the Romantic individual to exercise the cult that he frequently made of his own soul. The solitude and total freedom of the wilderness created a perfect setting for either melancholy or exultation.[28]

The European perception of nature and particularly Anglo-French ideas about primitivism got transferred to the New World, too. It became expressed in quite ambivalent pictures, overwhelmingly deriving from Christian thought.[29] Heaven and hell, garden versus wilderness, were the most common images deduced from this context. In the very early days of settlement, the wilderness image, however, dominated ideologically, for it offered convenient biblical connotations. It came to be seen as a testing ground for (the pioneers') faith, an opportunity to demonstrate their ability to withstand temptation. Early settlers perceived American nature as abundant Garden Eden, with Indians as children of innocence. This picture became reversed through Puritan mentality, and the Puritan villages symbolically turned into Christian strongholds, fending off the evils of wilderness. The Puritans regarded their settlements as fortresses of spirituality and civilization, surrounded by a vast landscape of sin, which was meant to be avoided. The indigenous inhabitants of this landscape functioned as negative counterparts in the Puritans' self-inflicted scenario about their history of settlement as a biblical play.[30] This scenario was also expressed in literary terms, mainly by war narratives and captivity narratives. It is important to mention that attitudes and beliefs of the various religious groups settling in America played a crucial part in approaching and treating its native inhabitants. Contrary to the Puritans, for whom "all Indians were victims beyond rescue of their low condition and that not much was to be gained by studying them,"[31] the Quakers, for instance, tried hard, although in vain, in their missionary attempts to Christianize Native Americans. Their passionate philosophy and, thus, their policy directed towards natives was not so much determined by dualisms such as civilization versus savagery.

Continual expansion and rapid settlement throughout the following centuries caused wilderness and all its implications to wane. The process of 'civilizing' the North American continent by exploring and, thus, taming nature's enigmatic character also incorporated the development of American Pastoralism. The idea of nature as a cultivated garden turned into a metaphor for the human potential of improvement and progress.[32] Methods of regaining something close to a 'paradisaic garden,' nevertheless, also yielded connotations of elitism:

> If there was a delicious melancholy for sophisticated and literary people in regretting the destruction of the primitive freedom of an untouched continent, the westward movement seemed to less imaginative observers a glorious victory of civilization over savagery and barbarism. For such people – and they were the vast majority – the Western hunter and guide was praiseworthy not because of his intrinsic wildness or half-savage glamour, but because he blazed trails that hard-working farmers could follow.[33]

Due to thorough discussions about the ideal model of mankind, several schools of thought, all interconnected with primitivism, sprang forth. Next to what is usually referred to as the progressivist stance, pastoralism is perhaps best known. Jeffersonian Agrarianism, for example, came to be seen as one particular variant of the pastoral concept. Also, Hector St. John de Crèvecoeur and his *Letters from an American Farmer* can be placed on a very simple level of the pastoral tradition.

The American wilderness, its exploration, plus the steady westward shift of the frontier did not only offer a prolific number of nature-culture images, but also stimulated the literary and academic discussions about them. The nature-culture dichotomy got perpetuated in American writing of any style and genre. The kaleidoscope of authors and texts involves Herman Melville, Nathaniel Hawthorne, and Walt Whitman, James Fenimore Cooper and dime novels, The Transcendentialists, Mark Twain, Helen Hunt Jackson, and Frederick Jackson Turner, Ernest Hemingway, William Faulkner, and Robert Frost.[34] A further investigation of primitivism in terms of American literature of the 19th and 20th century would be too extensive. Instead, new developments and trends in western society's perception and utilization of primitivism will be taken into consideration.

The succeeding analysis is an examination of the obvious correspondence between (anti)primitivism and the (ig)noble savage picture and an attempt to explain new developments in the dialectic relationship of civilization and savagism, which justify the prefix *neo*. This analysis of neo-primitivist tendencies is bound to the western hemisphere (i.e., North America – mainly the U.S. – and West and Central Europe). It is a west-east differential with trends and movements starting in the U.S. and, after certain intervals and due to the 'Americanization' of Europe, swamping to European countries as well.

(Anti)primitivism usually incorporates an (ig)noble savage image, functioning as a mirror image to the civilized citizen of society, the result being "that the savage is admired not merely for what he is, but for what he is not."[35] This image, then, becomes an expression of civilization's voids. Anything that is not an explicit integral part of civilization and its members at a particular time in history is projected upon savagism. This, for example, would include character traits or patterns of behavior, that either go against or beyond society's codex of do's and don'ts. Savagism turns into a valve for civilization and all its taboos. Until recently, western society's biggest taboo was the human body. Due to the dominating Christian tradition, bodily aspects of any form were denied and shunned. Supporters as well as critics of that tradition utilized primitive (wo)man to juxtapose the concept of civilized (Christian) life. For those in favor of civilization, the savage represented the heathen. This hereditary pagan exemplified a lustful and sinful creature, incapable of developing an awareness of its state of sin, much less repenting its wrongdoings and, thus, existing beyond salvation. The ignoble savage was born, purveying features that antiprimitivists perceived as negative and, subsequently, wanted to eradicate in modern man. Next to cannibalism, nakedness and promiscuity were the most commonly stressed among these features – and it was exactly the physical capacities that opponents and self-declared reformists of civilized society reveled in. They dignified savage people for a mythopoeic picture of physical and sexual freedom, based on "the desire to re-establish the paradisal state before the Fall, when sin did not yet exist and there was no conflict between the pleasures of the flesh and conscience."[36] The ennobled savages resulting from this perception were described in terms of beauty and naturalness of body, contradicting the restraints primitivists wanted to neutralize in the civilized system. Accordingly, most supporters of this picture would either not be aware of or ignore the fact that any (indigenous) culture lives and abides by a more or less subtle system of taboos.

The unequivocal visualization and interpretation of the (ig)noble savage according to physiognomy reiterated western civilization's denial and inhibition to 'become physical.' Officially, the sophisticated mind was supposed to dominate over the earthy body and not vice versa. This attitude has undergone a drastic change since the 1960s.[37] The iconoclastic picture of freely roaming bodies – if not superior to the mind, then, at least, equal to it – established by the sixties' counterculture, was not an entirely new invention. Richard Slotkin, for instance, stresses the intentionally repetitive scheme of the sixties' utilization of primitivism:

> "Countercultural" radicalism identified strongly with a rather traditional vision of the American Indians as the "Noble Savage" alternative to a civilization gone wrong. The iconography of beads and headbands, the adoption of "tribal" life-styles as a form of communalism untainted by political association with communism, the rationalization of drug use as a form of mystic religiosity, the linkage of political and ecological concerns, the withdrawal to wilderness refuges and the adoption of an outlaw or "renegade" stance toward the larger society – all of these phenomena so special to the sixties were acted out as if they were not innovative at all, but merely repetitions of an older pattern.[38]

The revolutionary impact, however, came with the succeeding (media) adaptation of primitivism. In the following decades, the human body became socially acceptable, and its social impact turned into a market factor. Suddenly, bodies would no longer be mere vessels of profanity, but means of public self-expression. The body as object of art and desire occupied any facet in western society's life. Slogans like 'mens sana in corpore sano' became increasingly postmodernized. Body art, expressed through piercing and tattooing, for instance, heavily started to plagiarize primitive motifs.

The media component in this development is a significant one, for mass media (television, billboards, magazines) became the pillars for conveying physical images. Once 'Nudity and Sex Sell' turned into a profitable motto, advertising would shower potential customers with images of naked bodies, the fashion, fitness, and cosmetics industries boomed. Any decade saw their fitness gurus. – The aerobics wave in the 1980s had Jane Fonda (who later admitted of having been bulimic at that time rather than thoroughly trained) as figurehead for an entire nation. The 1990s came up with Oprah Winfrey, who shared her secrets of weight loss with everyone, and plastic surgery became a 'normal' procedure to trim the outward appearance. Any celebrity, who would consider themselves particular, produced fitness videos and books about nutrition, dieting, and body shaping. 'Where do you work out?' became a standard phrase in any conversation, and self-declared adrenaline junkies would kill their increasing spare time by parachuting, scuba diving, and bungee jumping. Lately, the cosmetic industry would also zero in on men – after traditionally only singling out women – as new target groups for any anti-aging product to stay eternally young and beautiful.

Propagated beauty got commercially reinvented, so that any generation and any decade had their share of role models, and the alleged sexual revolution of the 1960s brought about an exhibition and scrutiny of physical aspects to the point of meaninglessness and superficiality. The emphasis on muscular, lean, and well-shaped bodies triggered an obsession with nutritional facts, dieting, and calorie counting amidst the background of evermore affluent food production and food resources. The post-World War II era changed from voluptuous-womanly bodies like Marilyn Monroe's, for example, to Twiggy- and Heroine-Chic-figures. The interrelation between wealth and body shape (as fertility images) has always been an evident one throughout history. The less food was available, the more body fat was fashionable and vice versa. Particular sorts of food like the potato, for instance, demonstrate that through a constant up and down of popularity, with heydays during famine and war times. Abundance of food, nowadays, determines the beauty image of slim, even skinny bodies. Anorexia nervosa/bulimia – as one particular variant of the 'Full Stomach Syndrome' – did not become famous as the Golden Girl Illness by mere chance. The once so popular fast food in the U.S. – as a specific sign of progress and technology, thus, civilization and even upward mobility – lost part of its appeal to health food, power food, and functional food. After World War II, ready-made food, frozen food, and TV dinners were turned into an icon of everyday life. As particular methods of processing and storing food were at that time considered to be indicators for a 'hygienic' household and, thus, a 'good' housekeeper (i.e., a socially efficient housewife), any diet that was not homegrown or homemade implied a particular form of economic wealth. Deep freezing, dehydrating, and canning food or adding stabilizers, preservatives, and artificial flavors or colors to it, stood for technological progress, the ability to afford buying such food for a certain form of luxury in a time when the menace of food shortage (or at least the memory of it) would still linger. This conception changed with the increasing availability and even overproduction of food. The mass production of food resulted in the consumers' daintiness and a renaissance of naturally/biologically grown food. Consuming comparatively uncontaminated food, nowadays, is to be regarded as a particular expression of sophistication and health awareness.

'Overfed,' 'oversexed,' and 'overtrained' like that, western civilization would soon feel the need for 'something spiritual' again. Society's voids in postmodernist, postfeminist, postcolonial, and post-Freudian times – while society at the same time being aware of the "controversial shiftiness of the prefix 'post'"[39] – show in the form of an emotional vacuum with traditional family structures collapsing, divorce rates and numbers of single households increasing. Traditional religions and churches seem too obsolete, orthodox, or institutional to meet the growing need for this 'something spiritual.' To most of their dissidents, these religious communities appear too static to address contemporary issues. Regarding this context, considerations about global political situations at the beginning of the 1990s are unavoidable. The initial enthusiasm about the end of the Cold War Era – with its possible nuclear threat being terminated or at least being minimized – got soon replaced by confusion and frustration about what came to be known as 'Cold Peace.' Post Cold War times did not prove to be safer or more peaceful (as originally expected), with geographical borders dissolving and, thus, disrupting habitual mental borders, the patterns of which could not easily be replaced. Although the hazard of a global war and nuclear holocaust seemed to be averted, the impression of instability rose with every new minor war that sprang forth, some in the middle of hypercivilized Europe. The chaos and cruelty of wartime situations, somehow happening at the doorsteps of the western world, reminded western society of the vulnerability and mortality of mankind in a very drastic way, which, again, deepened the longing for an emotional/spiritual stronghold.[40]

'Inner Emptiness' and 'Burned Out Syndrome' became standard vocabulary in defining society's anamnesis. Thus being diagnosed, the overwhelming majority of 'patients' wished to rejuvenate themselves in a physical as well as spiritual catharsis. Again, celebrities became *the* role-models for this catharsis. Madonna, for example, metamorphosed from a once self-staged enfant terrible and femme fatale into an overprotective mother, abandoning her Jean-Paul Gaultier bra in favor of spiritual/cultural 'trinkets.' Her colleague, Alanis Morissette, would humbly backpack through India to meditate upon fame and financial success.

For this search of 'inner balance,' primitivism and, naturally, the noble savage image came in handy. Whereas former generations had predominantly resorted to this image to escape from physical inhibitions of civilization's corset, contemporary society provided this image with an entirely new nuance: the spiritual noble savage, demonstrating outer (i.e., with the environment) and inner (i.e., with oneself) harmony. The beginnings of this new perception of the noble savage can be roughly placed at the divide between the 1980s and the 1990s, which also corresponds with the shift towards primitive spirituality in the New Age movement. Finally, the traditionally plagiarized Indian nobility of physical aesthetics, bravery, and stoicism became enhanced by a new catch phrase: the spiritual, wise, and prophetic Indian. As a consequence, the 1990s – after centuries of physical pet Indianness – innovated savage figures by having them endorse mind/spirit qualities and talents.

This *neo*-noble savage is characterized by an inner strength and glowing, which is not – and this is particularly interesting – so much due to mental, but emotional knowledge.[41] Traditionally, the savage's mental capacity for analytical reasoning has never been a genuine part in philosophical, religious, or political debates.[42] Also today's emphasis on strictly non-intellectual/non-academic/non-scientific feelings and instincts is a crucial one, for it does not only represent civilization's evermore denial of the savage mind (be it noble or ignoble) for any cerebral ability, but also expresses contemporary society's unease with institutionalized education and learned facts. The flood of information of the so-called data highway, offered by the Internet and dozens of TV channels, is compensated by the noble savage's 'wisdom' and 'prophetic' knowledge. Therefore, the noble savage turns into a keeper of spiritual secrets and truisms, providing remedies for any of society's ills in a high-speed, high-tech world. This neo-primitivist rationale, once again, popularizes Indians as pre-Columbian and ancient by having them resemble pure common sense, devoid of any sophisticated rationality.

Although undoubtedly tenuous, this neo-noble Indian phenotype has also reached its pinnacle with various methods of playing Indian in the 1990s. Indian wannabes and outalooks do not only roam the streets of Santa Fe and Sedona any longer. Visual and spiritual demands of Indianness are not merely limited to the market branch of tourism with the sale of 'genuine' Indian jewelry and dolls, but expands to everyday life as well. This "imperialist nostalgia"[43] – as having always been manifestly evident in bogus books and summer camps, for instance – nowadays turns the neo-noble Indian into a cultural icon. The imperialist factor is a central one, for this utilization of Indianness cannot help but remain a strictly ethnocentric one. The focus is not so much on a realistic interest in Native American culture, but rather on an abstract appropriation of stereotypical Indian images and life styles.

The result is an implicitly chauvinist attitude, benevolent towards the alien Other only for a personal interest. This benevolence towards Indianness, usually colored by an elegiac mood, perpetuates erroneous as well as detrimental assumptions about the Other. This Other becomes subordinated to a self-proclaimed philanthropy, that rigorously omits whatever does not fit into or correspond with the scheme of Indianness. Playing Indian via neo-primitivism has developed into "a vogue lifestyle for the social elite"[44] and into a means to mollify their 'Full Stomach Syndrome.' The plethora of shaman workshops and sweat hut seminars, with so-called pipe carriers instructing and monitoring eager Indians-to-be, exemplifies the popular image of the spiritually and visually ravishing Indian. This "spiritual supermarket"[45] may be tendentious in the eyes of some critics – native and non-native alike – however, this does not prevent it from being utterly successful in the western world.

The succeeding chapter is an analysis of the most recent consumerist escapism to the neo-noble Indians' world. Neo-primitivist Indianness – as a particular form of "runaway individualism"[46] – has been on a tremendous rise since the 1990s, especially solidifying as a forum for distributing esoteric remedies on a larger scale. Accordingly, this esoteric pilfering of neo-primitive wisdom and spiritual power can be regarded as a substratum for white shamanism.

Notes

1. The hazardously discriminative patterns of positive stereotyping are particularly evident in statements by wannabe Indians. Self-declared 'friends of the Indian' describe their portrayals of ennobled savages as emphatically helpful in breaking down barriers between cultures. In fact, the presumption of the noble savage contributes to the vicious circle of stereotypes in the same way as the ignoble one does.

2. Robert F. Berkhofer Jr., *The White Man's Indian: Images of the American Indian from Columbus to the Present* (New York: Vintage Books, 1979), 13.

3. The dualism between savage and civilized environment and its significance for white shaman writing (e.g., the reservation as idealized landscape and shaman's retreat) will be further examined in the succeeding chapter.

4. Columbus' so-called My-Man-Friday Syndrome is thoroughly discussed by Tzvetan Todorov. Cf. Tzvetan Todorov, *The Conquest of America: The Question of the Other*, trans. Richard Howard (Paris: Editions du Seuil, 1982; New York: HarperPerennial, 1992). – Language in general has always been an intrinsic part of imperialism and colonization, since it functions as a means to

establish the culture of the conqueror and, thus, to dominate and control also the mental/linguistic patterns of the dominated. For an analysis of language and colonization, see also Eric Cheyfitz, *The Poetics of Imperialism: Translation and Colonization from "The Tempest" to "Tarzan"* (New York and Oxford: Oxford University Press, 1991).

5. Daniel Defoe's *Robinson Crusoe*, though a subtle satire on the dualism of civilization versus savagism, still, exemplifies European perceptions of natives as foremost being labor forces. As *liberté, égalité, fraternité* has only been applied to the *myth* of the noble savage – so Stelio Cro – there has never been a realistic basis for a mutually equal interaction between Europeans and non-Europeans. Cf. Stelio Cro, *The Noble Savage: Allegory of Freedom* (Waterloo, Ontario: Wilfrid Laurier University Press, 1990).

The history of the Cherokee tribe, for example, assimilating intellectually as well as materially to the European settlers, shows this fact particularly well. – Further details on the Cherokees' story can be found in the following chapter.

In *Spider Woman's Granddaughters*, Paula Gunn Allen also comments on white policies to turn natives into servants and restrict them to this role. Her example are the boarding schools, educating Native Americans not to become literate, but merely obedient. Cf. Paula Gunn Allen, introduction to *Spider Woman's Granddaughters: Traditional Tales and Contemporary Writing by Native American Women*, ed. Paula Gunn Allen (New York: Fawcett Columbine, 1990), 1-25.

6. The initial phase of (the Spanish) conquest of the Americas, for example, incorporated the conquistadores' attitude to classify and determine the savages' status (as compared to Europeans). Prior to missionizing natives, questions of whether or not they even had souls to be rescued and of whether their 'animalistic state' prevailed had to be solved. After they had been found worthy of salvation, Christianity became a means to express what savagism lacked. Therefore, Christianity was a primal factor in establishing the civilization-savagism dichotomy. The conversion of natives, in some cases, even turned into a legitimation of massacring them, since their souls had been saved in advance.

7. Scott B. Vickers, *Native American Identities: From Stereotype to Archetype in Art and Literature* (Albuquerque: University of New Mexico Press, 1998), 104.

8. The analysis and evaluation of stereotypes connected to Euro-American perception and treatment of America's native inhabitants has become an increasingly popular issue in academic writing. Any author dealing with specific Native American topics focuses on particular parameters of the noble-ignoble savage dichotomy. Jean-Jacques Simard, for instance, summarizes the three most crucial characteristics of such stereotypes, calling them *monolithic images, logically obverse twin images*, and *images representing archetypes*. Cf. Jean-Jacques Simard, "White Ghosts, Red Shadows: The Reduction of North American Natives," in *The Invented Indian: Cultural Fictions and Government Policies*, ed. James A. Clifton (New Brunswick, NJ, and London: Transaction Publishers, 1996), 333-69.

9. As is frequently argued, Native American tribes, their languages, and cultures were so variable in times of European discovery that some tribes associated more easily with Europeans (for example, over the question of torture) than with fellow tribes. The Pan-Indian Movement, starting in the 1960s, has given way to a more unified approach to Native American issues and a more 'collective' feeling of Native American identity among most tribes.

10. The question of 'What does an Indian look like?' is frequently raised by Native Americans to work against common stereotypical visions. Debra L. Merskin and Devon A. Mihesuah are only two in a row of Native American academics to address this issue, the latter one also involving the aspect of 'blood quantum' as a means to verify 'true' Indians.

The idea of various degrees of Indian blood, recently, has become revived in a quite problematic context. Due to white inclinations towards having 'a drop of Indian blood' in their veins (for idealistic or quite materialistic reasons – meaning the access to gambling-tax-free land and, thus, the opportunity to build or run a casino), the racist concept of blood quantum is more prevalent than ever. In addition to that, it still happens that (particularly European) tourists complain about not seeing 'real' Indians whenever they visit a reservation, while (modern) Native Americans stand right next to them.

11. 'Costumes' is a presumptuous word, often earning scorn by Native Americans. Instead of the more appropriate terms 'outfit' or 'regalia' (at powwows), the word 'costume' implies 'carnival,' having nothing to do with Native American identity, but rather with a white interpretation of Indian entertainment.

12. For a study on Catlin's perception of Indians, see Brian W. Dippie, *The Vanishing American: White Attitudes and U.S. Indian* Policy (Lawrence: University Press of Kansas, 1982). For a discussion of Catlin's image symbolism, see also Klaus Lubbers, *Born for the Shade: Stereotypes of the Native American in United States Literature and the Visual Arts, 1776-1894* (Amsterdam and Atlanta: Rodopi, 1994), especially 155-61.

13. Alison Griffiths, "Science and Spectacle: Native American Representation in Early Cinema," in *Dressing in Feathers: The Construction of the Indian in American Popular Culture,* ed. S. Elizabeth Bird (Boulder, CO, and Oxford: Westview Press, 1998), 88.

14. John C. Ewers, "The Static Images," in *The Pretend Indians: Images of Native Americans in the Movies*, eds. Gretchen M. Bataille and Charles L. P. Silet (Ames: Iowa State University Press, 1980), 17.

15. Louise K. Barnett, *The Ignoble Savage: American Literary Racism 1790-1890* (Westport, CT, and London: Greenwood Press, 1975), 107.

The assumption of the stoic Indian, when it comes to torturing and pain, is also implied in the German language through the phrase 'Ein Indianer kennt keinen Schmerz,' translating something like 'An Indian knows no pain.' This phrase is frequently used with children when they hurt themselves. – An example that proves the everyday-like character of stereotypes and their conditioning impact on young minds. For a thorough analysis of prejudices concerning Indianness amongst children/young adults in Germany, see

Hartmut Lutz, *"Indianer" und "Native Americans:" Zur sozial- und literarhistorischen Vermittlung eines Stereotyps* (Hildesheim, Zurich, and New York: Georg Olms Verlag, 1985).

16. Donald L. Kaufmann, "The Indian As Media Hand-Me-Down," in *The Pretend Indians: Images of Native Americans in the Movies*, eds. Gretchen M. Bataille and Charles L. P. Silet (Ames: Iowa State University Press, 1980), 30. Another commonly known representative of the mute Indian is Chief Bromden. Ken Kesey deliberately plays on the image of the silent, victimized Indian by having Bromden only *pretend* to be mute. Nevertheless, towards the end of the novel, Chief Bromden's character is somewhat ennobled through his single escape from the asylum.

17. Those movies somehow mirror John Wayne's private opinion about Indians as being 'selfish' for trying 'to keep the land to themselves.' In the movie *Smoke Signals*, Wayne's attitude is subtly hinted at through the song about his teeth, performed by the two protagonists, who are banned to the back of a bus (which, again, is another classic hint at Rosa Parks) for the mere reason of being native. Cf. *Smoke Signals*, directed by Chris Eyre (Miramax/ShadowCatcher, 1998).
For a study of the development of Indian plots and figures from silent to contemporary films, see Michael Hilger, *From Savage to Nobleman: Images of Native Americans in Film* (Lanham, MD, and London: Scarecrow Press, 1995).

18. John E. O'Connor, "The White Man's Indian: An Institutional Approach," in *Hollywood's Indian: The Portrayal of the Native American in Film*, eds. Peter C. Rollins and John E. O'Connor (Lexington: University Press of Kentucky, 1998), 37.

19. Devon A. Mihesuah, *American Indians: Stereotypes and Realities* (Atlanta and Regina: Clarity Press, 1998), 115. – Cf. *Black Robe*, directed by Bruce Beresford (Samuel Goldwyn, 1991).
For profound analyses, dealing with TV shows and the representation of Indianness, see Annette M. Taylor "Cultural Heritage in *Northern Exposure*," and S. Elizabeth Bird "Not My Fantasy: The Persistence of Indian Imagery in *Dr. Quinn, Medicine Woman*," both in *Dressing in Feathers: The Construction of the Indian in American Popular Culture*, ed. S. Elizabeth Bird (Boulder, CO, and Oxford: Westview Press, 1998), 229-44; 245-61.

20. Robert Baird, "'Going Indian': *Dances with Wolves* (1990)," in *Hollywood's Indian: The Portrayal of the Native American in Film*, eds. Peter C. Rollins and John E. O'Connor (Lexington: University Press of Kentucky, 1998), 160. – Cf. *Dances with Wolves*, directed by Kevin Costner (Orion Pictures, 1990) and *Little Big Man*, directed by Arthur Penn (Fox, 1970).

21. Marianna Torgovnick, *Primitive Passions: Men, Women, and the Quest for Ecstasy* (New York: Alfred A. Knopf, 1997), 139-40.

22. For a study on the archetypal character of primitivist scenery, see Charles L. Sandford, *The Quest for Paradise: Europe and the American Moral Imagination* (Urbana: University of Illinois Press, 1961).

23. Arthur O. Lovejoy and George Boas, *Primitivism and Related Ideas in Antiquity* (Baltimore and London: Johns Hopkins University Press, 1997), 7.

24. George Boas, *Primitivism and Related Ideas in the Middle Ages* (Baltimore and London: Johns Hopkins University Press, 1997), 97. For a discourse on the Wild Man, specifically, see Richard Bernheimer, *Wild Men in the Middle Ages: A Study in Art, Sentiment, and Demonology* (Cambridge, Mass.: Harvard University Press, 1952). For a discussion of remythifications in terms of Wild Man formulas, see Edward Dudley and Maximillian E. Novak, eds., *The Wild Man within: An Image in Western Thought from the Renaissance to Romanticism* (London: University of Pittsburgh Press, 1972).

25. Christopher B. Steiner, "Travel Engravings and the Construction of the Primitive," in *Prehistories of the Future: The Primitivist Project and the Culture of Modernism*, eds. Elazar Barkan and Ronald Bush (Stanford: Stanford University Press, 1995), 203.

26. Leo Marx, *The Machine in the Garden: Technology and the Pastoral Ideal in America* (London, Oxford, and New York: Oxford University Press, 1974), 65.

27. Benjamin Keen, *The Aztec Image in Western Thought* (New Brunswick, NJ: Rutgers University Press, 1971), 217-18; Keen's emphasis.

28. Roderick Nash, *Wilderness and the American Mind*, 3rd ed. (New Haven and London: Yale University Press, 1982), 47.

29. For a study of Christian imagology interconnected with perceptions of nature, see George H. Williams, *Wilderness and Paradise in Christian Thought: The Biblical Experience of the Desert in the History of Christianity and the Paradise Theme in the Theological Idea of the University* (New York: Harper and Brothers, 1962).

30. The Puritans' (and especially Cotton Mather's) attitude towards and treatment of Indians has been theorized in a prolific number of academic works. See, for instance, Richard Slotkin, *Regeneration through Violence: The Mythology of the American Frontier, 1600-1860* (Middletown, CT: Wesleyan University Press, 1979) and Annette Kolodny, *The Lay of the Land: Metaphor As Experience and History in American Life and Letters* (Chapel Hill: University of North Carolina Press, 1975). Kolodny's analysis of the interrelationship between femininity images and reports about the American landscape is particularly interesting, for it demonstrates the periodicity of pro-culture/anti-nature times, mirrored in perceptions/descriptions of women and savages alike.

31. Roy Harvey Pearce, *Savagism and Civilization: A Study of the Indian and the American Mind* (Berkeley, Los Angeles, and London: University of California Press, 1988), 25.

32. For an analysis of *the garden* as product of parables and myths, see Harry Levin, *The Myth of the Golden Age in the Renaissance* (Bloomington and London: Indiana University Press, 1969).

33. Henry Nash Smith, *Virgin Land: The American West As Symbol and Myth* (Cambridge, Mass., and London: Harvard University Press, 1982), 52-53.

34. For reviews about literary depictions of the savage image, see Albert Keiser, *The Indian in American Literature* (New York: Oxford University

Press, 1933) and Leslie A. Fiedler, *The Return of the Vanishing American* (New York: Stein and Day Publishers, 1968).

35. Hoxie Neale Fairchild, *The Noble Savage: A Study in Romantic Naturalism* (New York: Russell and Russell, 1961), 8.

36. Mircea Eliade, *The Sacred and the Profane: The Nature of Religion*, trans. Willard R. Trask (Hamburg: Rowohlt Verlag, 1957; San Diego, New York, and London: Harcourt Brace, 1987), 207.

37. For discussions of the sixties' element of self-fulfillment, see Peter Clecak, *America's Quest for the Ideal Self: Dissent and Fulfillment in the 60s and 70s* (New York and Oxford: Oxford University Press, 1983) and Morris Dickstein, *Gates of Eden: American Culture in the Sixties* (Cambridge, Mass., and London: Harvard University Press, 1997).

38. Richard Slotkin, *The Fatal Environment: The Myth of the Frontier in the Age of Industrialization 1800-1890* (New York: Atheneum, 1985), 17.

39. Homi K. Bhabha, *The Location of Culture* (London and New York: Routledge, 1994), 1.

40. For a study of socio- and religio-affirmative developments in belief-systems, see Peter L. Berger, Brigitte Berger, and Hansfried Kellner, *The Homeless Mind: Modernization and Consciousness* (New York: Random House, 1973).

41. So-called emotional knowledge also shows a significant correspondence between commonly socialized gender and ethnicity. Usually – when it comes to 'genderizing' knowledge – women are socially coded as obtaining higher emotional capabilities and a weaker left/logic brain hemisphere activity. Interestingly enough, the neo-noble (male) Indian is also 'effeminated' in most cases. For a discussion of the so-called 'Indian beau,' see Peter van Lent, "'Her Beautiful Savage': The Current Sexual Image of the Native American Male," in *Dressing in Feathers: The Construction of the Indian in American Popular Culture*, ed. S. Elizabeth Bird (Boulder, CO, and Oxford: Westview Press, 1998), 211-27.

42. For an analysis of classic assumptions about this 'docta ignorantia,' see Kurt Goldstein, "Concerning the Concept of 'Primitivity,'" in *Culture in History: Essays in Honor of Paul Radin*, ed. Stanley Diamond (New York: Columbia University Press, 1960), 99-117.

43. Renato Rosaldo, *Culture and Truth: The Remaking of Social Analysis* (Boston: Beacon Press, 1993), 68-87.

44. Theodore S. Jojola, "*Moo Mesa*: Some Thoughts on Stereotypes and Image Appropriation," in *Dressing in Feathers: The Construction of the Indian in American Popular Culture*, ed. S. Elizabeth Bird (Boulder, CO, and Oxford: Westview Press, 1998), 264.

45. Michael Castro, *Interpreting the Indian: Twentieth-Century Poets and the Native American* (Albuquerque: University of New Mexico Press, 1983; Norman and London: University of Oklahoma Press, 1991), 157.

46. Philip J. Deloria, *Playing Indian* (New Haven and London: Yale University Press, 1998), 170.

Part I

1. White Shamanism

Indeed, today it is popular to be an Indian. Within a decade it may be a necessity.
Vine Deloria Jr., *Red Earth, White Lies: Native Americans and the Myth of Scientific Fact*

But champions of the vitality and integrity of Native American traditions are not necessarily in favor of multiculturalism.
Arnold Krupat, *The Turn to the Native: Studies in Criticism and Culture*

The following passages are intended to make the genealogy and consolidation of white shamanism more transparent. The 1990s turned into a prism for New Agean equivocations on shamanism. Moreover, perimeters like 'Caucasian' and 'civilized' altered into a bedrock for esoteric shamanism, which would quickly establish itself within the neo-primitivist periphery. A brief chronology of the development of the term white shamanism is supposed to explain, first of all, the makeshift of the attribute 'white.' Secondly, it also aims at clarifying the frequent usage of white shamanism as collective term for the 1990s' phantasmagoria of esoteric Indianness.

Further, white shamanism is examined in terms of its Janus-faced character. Namely, this particular variant of playing Indian by white rules incites aspects far beyond assimilative patterns. At the core of white shamanism, there linger strategies of postcolonial paternalism. This means that going native in white shaman style does not so much evolve from an essential urge for 'Indianization.' The emphasis, rather, is on 'out-Indianing' genuine Native Americans through spiritual retribalization.

One of the newest masterpieces of playing Indian piety is the endorsement of shamanism. The concept of the 'shaman' has turned into a notorious foray for a prolific number of people, particularly artists of any kind. The cutting edge for the revived interest in this concept is a touch of haughty reserve and distinctiveness, that a slew of people vividly associates with the term shaman. The image of the shaman as guide, prophet, adviser for their tribe got readily snapped up and grabbed on to by people, who would consider their work, beliefs, and lives as chefs-d'oeuvre of this image. The principle of the shaman, being a central person for a group of people, undoubtedly, is a very attractive and tempting axiom for the general public. Applied to art in particular, this principle, however, could never amount to be anything else but imitative. Comparable to symptoms of psychological introjection – since white Indianness is "apparently only accessible through acting, impersonation, and/or acquisition"[1] – appropriations of shamanism remain within the borders of reproductive and cliche-ridden patterns. Thus, shamanism is viewed in a very undifferentiated, oversimplified way, otherwise it would not fit into this patterned contrivance.

In most cases, the focus of any postmodern perception of shamanism is placed on Indians. Any Indian product, for instance, workshops, books, jewelry, and videos, on the esoteric market is usually inundated with predominantly white appropriations of Indian shamanism. As the shaman is considered to be special and, thus, pivotal in a community, this figure turns into a welcome placebo for civilization's anguish about its community. The feeling of being powerful, influential, wise, and respected is implicitly immanent to the wannabe shaman attitude. In *Patterns of Culture*, Ruth Benedict, analyzing tribes of the American Northwest Coast, describes the 'job' of the shaman as both privileged and deriving from supernatural powers.[2] It is exactly those features that hoax shamans are so fond of and strive for. The privileges allow the shaman to reprimand and enlighten the community, and the supernatural aura justifies and legitimates this absolutistic behavior – or so it is assumed.

Originally, the genuine shaman concept is as complicated as ancient. Etymologically, the term shaman has nothing to do with Native American, but Siberian languages – more precisely even, the Tungusic expression *šaman*, as discussed by Mircea Eliade.[3] Although it is true that the shaman always held a pungent position in society, it did not necessarily have to be an entirely positive and unproblematic one. The shaman could be assertive or peevish up to the point of being schizophrenic. In a pop scholarly approach, Peter Farb caricatures the shaman figure by overemphasizing their hostile nature: "The person who becomes a shaman is almost always more misanthropic, more covertly aggressive, and less physically skilled than the ordinary man."[4] The privileges, certainly, involved a high amount of responsibility and devotion. The respect of the entire community had to be gained and adhered to, most of the time not so much by supernatural means but by techniques of cause and effect (i.e., prediction and happening).

The shaman, offering creative as well as holistic cures to the needs of the collective, is a popular contemporary notion. Combining the gifts of artist and psychotherapist in one person, this image-laden shaman should treat civilization's psychosomatic diseases. Their task would be to restore civilization's disrupted balance – physically *and* spiritually. Consequently, the germane shamanic idea of any illness resulting from the so-called 'rape of the soul,' originally paraphrased in Central and North Asia, becomes modified for current market factors.[5]

Since the beginning of the 1980s, white shamanism has galvanized a mainstream phenomenon of esoteric Indianness. The omnipresence of the term white shaman, or simply shaman, in literary circles and circles of literary criticism alike needs to be investigated concerning use and abuse. Originally, the term white shaman was invented by Native American poets and writers such as Wendy Rose, Leslie Marmon Silko, and Geary Hobson, to label white writers, particularly poets, who panegyrized Indianness and (Indian) shamanism in the 1970s. By referring to themselves as shamans, poets like, for instance, Gene Fowler or Jim Cody, adopted a new way to stigmatize Indianness. Geary Hobson, calling white shamanism a new form of cultural imperialism, defines the term white shaman as follows: "These are the apparently growing number of small-press poets of generally white, Euro-Christian American background, who in their poems assume the persona of the shaman, usually in the guise of an American Indian medicine man."[6]

While initially deconstructive terms, created by Native Americans to criticize white idolatry of Indianness, white shaman(ism) – as the 1980s unfolded – permeated the white community in question. Thus, these basically derogatory terms got snatched up by white artists, particularly writers, to delineate their work. Unlike their predecessors in the 1960s, who would come up with a fake Indian identity to attract the public, wannabe Indians of the 1980s managed the squaring of the circle. They did not at all deny their white, urban background, but explicitly stressed this fact in every interview about or preface to their books. Being aware of the dreadful faux pas of former bogus writers, they quickly learned to abandon their imaginative Indian ancestors in favor of a purely white heritage. The message they got across by doing so was something like this: 'Hey, we might be white, still, we have been capable of becoming Indian (i.e., white shamans) in spirit.' Statements like these, supposedly, should serve as shield to aggravating criticism. Since the 1980s' society – having learned from previous deceptions of Apple Indians – was more aware of frauds and charlatans, the term white shaman came in handy to practice Indian charades without the hazard of losing credibility in the eyes of the reading public.

So far, white shamanism is the last entity in a myriad of texts, employing Indiannes in terms of what Robert F. Berkhofer Jr. has referred to as "the professionalization of philanthropy."[7] The significance of white books about Indianness is their accordance with public taste at any particular time, showing a slow but gradual process from the Indian as mere object for white encounters with the primitive and white curiosity about the exotic alien to a by no means less stereotyping white reverence for Indianness as substitute culture. Whenever one particular way of utilizing the Indian Other shows a certain degree of saturation through the sales figures on the book market, white authors resort to new ways of attracting readers and keeping them interested for a while. The earliest phases of this book production have been characterized by a particular form of *contact zone* between whites and Indians. Mary Louise Pratt's model of the *contact zone,* though emphasizing the absence of "separateness or apartheit," provides one significantly interesting aspect for the discussion of white/Native American encounters on the territory of literature, which is the "radically asymmetrical relations of power."[8] Initiated and pushed through by the white counterpart, this form of contact zone has almost exclusively been one-sided. Early white-Native American co-operation on texts – predominantly oral literature being recorded and translated – has always taken place through the preconditioned constellation of white professional (i.e., anthropologist/ethnographer) and Indian storyteller/voice of the past.[9] The white professional, befriending and promoting their Indian source, thereby holding the part of the guardian and advocator, has continued with the tradition of coauthored books. Since the general interest is always placed on Indian life (perceived as being tremendously different from white existence), most of these coauthored books turned out to be biographies. Biographies, produced by Indian friends,[10] have always enjoyed great popularity – the implication being that an Indian by themselves is not literate enough to write their story.

Also university presses support the genre of the 'Indian life story,' a fact that makes this genre particularly susceptible to ambiguity. This ambiguity invades the Native American (academic) world as well: university editorial boards, dealing with Indian editions and involving well-known Native American academics and writers, coexist with dubious institutions, bringing forth unauthorized biographical accounts. The most famous example for the latter is John G. Neihardt's *Black Elk Speaks*. Black Elk's disavowal of this account is hardly known by the general public.[11] Generally, quasiautobiographies like these contribute to the everlasting popularity of Indian storyteller cliches.

Lakota Woman is another example of how Indian life stories become unilaterally exploited by the (media) public. It is the first in a trilogy of books about "the Crow Dog life stories (Mary Moore's and Leonard Crow Dog's stories of the Wounded Knee Uprising of 1973) written by another transplanted European who now lives in New York, an Indian expert and Hungarian/Austrian photographer named Richard Erdoes."[12] Concerning the media aspect, the three books (i.e., *Lakota Woman*, 1991; *Ohitika Woman*, 1994; *Crow Dog: Four Generations of Sioux Medicine Men*, 1996) have also been turned into television movies.

Selling off Indian lives is nothing new. Perhaps the best-known case of a 'traditional' Indian, coping with western civilization by and large, is Ishi, the so-called last Yahi. After having been caught as the last of the Yana, a tribe isolated from civilization, Ishi spent the rest of his life – from 1911 to 1916 – as live sensation under the protectorate of Alfred Kroeber. As he was last of his kind and, thus, the embodiment of the vanishing race, Ishi quickly turned into an attraction for anthropologists and newspaper people alike. Ishi's discovery fell into a time when Indians, more and more, became targets for white acts of either charity or self-fulfillment. Artists of any kind retrofit their work, embracing Indians and Indian culture as *muses* for an inspiration beyond and against western society. Painters and writers, for instance, exiled themselves in communities, later to be known as 'Taos colonies.'[13] While the Santa Fe and Taos colonies also promoted Native American potters, weavers, and carvers to exhibit their art, Native American writers of that time remained widely unknown to the public. Since literacy, next to proprietorship and separatism, equaled civilization, writers did not so much attract and/or please white entrepreneurs of Indianness.[14] After all, at that time they did by no means represent the typical Indian. Above all, compared to 'ordinary' Indians, some of them kept an alienated position by descending from sometimes wealthy, sometimes part white families as well as from white school and university systems. Writers, ranging from Charles A. Eastman and Mourning Dove (Christine Quintasket) to John M. Oskison, John Joseph Mathews, and D'Arcy McNickle – reflecting critically and differentially on white-native as well as native-native relations – implicitly paved the way for the post-Momaday era of writers. Alfred Kroeber's wife, Theodora, also (co)edited a series of books dealing with Ishi's life story from primitive man to civilization's pet (i.e., *Ishi in Two Worlds*, 1961; *Ishi, Last of His Tribe*, 1964; *Ishi, the Last Yahi*, 1979). The first releases of these books correlate with the heyday of Indianness in the 1960s. The sixties' and seventies' fascination with Indianness manifested itself in an abundant number of novels, published and republished: *Indian Summer* (John Knowles), *The Man Who Killed the Deer* (Frank Waters), *Cherokee Woman* (Francis Dave), *Give Me Wind* (Jan Jordan), *Odette* (Reuben Berkovitch), *Laughing Boy* (Oliver La Farge), *When the Legends Die* (Hal Borland), *Seven Arrows* (Hyemeyohsts Storm), *The Education of Little Tree* (Forrest Carter).

These authors pursued quite different intentions with their novels and, accordingly, triggered quite different critical responses. The process of evaluating and reevaluating some of these novels continues up until today. Novels functioning as "vehicle for social criticism,"[15] for example, have been met with comparatively mild contempt over the years, whereas those that turned out to be bogus books are criticized vociferously. It is important to stress, however, that today's discussion of these novels is, still, merely limited to a relatively small group of 'insiders' being familiar with the matter, while the vast reading public is unaware of newly discovered historical and biographical evidence about this literature and/or its authors. The predominantly scholarly debates, however, are characterized by quite dissimilar attitudes when it comes to less obscure writers like Frank Waters, Oliver La Farge, or Hal Borland, for example. Frank Waters is generally regarded as the most credible of these authors. Vine Deloria Jr. – usually being one of the fiercest critics of non-native writers dealing with Indianness – compiled a very favorable book about Frank Waters, called *Frank Waters: Man and Mystic*.[16] Waters literary works, originally written in the 1930s and 1940s, became tremendously popular and, thus, republished in the 1960s. Although some Hopi communities feel animosity towards Waters for collaborating with Hopi elders on *The Book of the Hopi*, his books, sometimes fictional, sometimes autobiographical, are more authentic in terms of anthropological information and less awkward in style than those of other writers. Next to Frank Waters, only Oliver La Farge comes close to these standards. Concerning Hal Borland, however, the situation is less clear. Borland's Bildungsroman *When the Legends Die* produced the most divergent reactions from native and non-native critics. Elémire Zolla emphasized the *Legends* highly formalized style and its "mimesis of native poetic inwardness."[17] Michael Dorris, analyzing the *Legends* beyond style, placed Borland in a row of writers, imitating Indianness unsuccessfully.[18] This view is radically opposed by Vine Deloria Jr. in *God Is Red*, mentioning *Legends* together with Momaday's *House Made of Dawn* as "few successful novels about modern Indian life."[19]

Moving on to the group of bogus books/writers, the matter gets even more complicated. Bogus in this context means 'pretend,' signifying either stories that have been sold as authentic record of Indianness (i.e., bogus books) or authors calling themselves Indians when, in fact, they were not (i.e., bogus writers). Carlos Castaneda is responsible for the most famous bogus books, the Don Juan books. Castaneda made use of the sixties' 'guru mania.' The sixties' counterculture was particularly fond of utilizing non-European cultures and religions for the purpose of gaining a 'higher sensibility' in life. 'Finding one's path' was a common slogan, and people started to look for teachers or masters as well as drugs that might lead them to this path of psychedelic experience. One of the most notorious 'gurus' in this respect was Don Juan, who, after years of praise and idealization, turned out to be a mere invention by Carlos Castaneda. Castaneda's books about Don Juan's 'teachings' proved to be highly successful in the 1960s, even earning him a Ph.D. in anthropology. The unmasking of Don Juan, the alleged Yaqui elder, as a mere fictional figure triggered a controversial debate about the credibility of Castaneda's writings, which has not subsided ever since. Despite negative evaluation of and press – the first article appearing as early as 1973 in *Time* – about the Don Juan series, semiacademic authors continue to refer to Castaneda as 'serious' source, as, for instance, Fritjof Capra in *Uncommon Wisdom: Conversations with Remarkable People* and Jack D. Forbes in his polemic *Columbus and Other Cannibals*. While authors and literary critics widely included the Don Juan books in their literary analyses, dealing with Native American Studies in the 1960s – like, for example, Elémire Zolla in *The Writer and the Shaman: A Morphology of the American Indian* – the books, today, are a target for heavy criticism. David Murray, for example, stresses the impact of Don Juan books on "a generation of students" looking for "answers and alternatives to the impasse of logic and rationality reached in their own repressively rational society."[20] Also Richard de Mille's approach to Castaneda's books is a particularly interesting one, for it contributes useful aspects to the ongoing debate of whether these fictional texts can be used to exemplify abstract literary thoughts. By applying the terms *authenticity* and *validity*, de Mille differentiates between several ways of deciphering the text. By classifying Castaneda's writing as *valid-inauthentic*, de Mille concludes:

> Scientists need to know whether they are dealing with credible or non-credible reporters. "Is this writer a liar?" is neither a trivial question nor one that should be evaded by appeals to the ineffability of mystical experience, the universality of phenomena, cultural diffusion, the truthfulness of novels, or the problem of subjectivity in the philosophy of science. It is a question scientists must sometimes ask if they don't wish to be let astray.[21]

The most severe case of bogus writers is unquestioningly Forrest Carter. His *Education of Little Tree*, published as autobiography, depicting a childhood with Cherokee grandparents, has been revealed as perhaps the biggest hoax in the tradition of wannabe Indian writers. There is ample evidence that Forrest Carter was a pseudonym for Asa Earl ('Ace') Carter, who was neither orphaned as little boy (as described in *Little Tree*) nor raised by grandparents, much less Cherokee people. Carter's activities as segregationist and member of the North Alabama White Citizens Council are equally proved, and, although not explicitly documented, his leadership of a Ku Klux Klan branch is no longer doubted. The list of criticism about Carter and his bogus book seems endless, but, despite all these well-known facts, *The Education of Little Tree* enjoys great popularity among readers (kids *and* adults) and even appears on reading lists in classes on Native American Literature. The generation of writers succeeding this bogus era has learned from the mistakes of pretend Indians. Since scandals about identity and ethnic background could turn out to be subversive to popularity *and* profit margin on the literary market, fictional Indian ancestors and princesses became quickly abandoned in favor of a purely Wasp heritage. People like Ruth Beebe Hill, for example, explicitly stressed their essentially white background, while at the same time appropriating Indianness for their writing. Hill, of course, being far from practicing white shamanism, nevertheless, holds the position of what could be called a 'transition author,' by anticipating an all-white-Mayflower-forefather-myth attitude. Hill's *Hanta Yo*, published in 1979, is prototypical for the genre of books emerging in the 1980s and 1990s. Though Ruth Beebe Hill – as compared to white shamans – is not so much concerned with an Indian guru/teacher instructing her on Indianness, she presents her novel as result of gathering and translating anthropological and historical information from her Dakota informant Chunksa Yuha. Originally heavily promoted and applauded, *Hanta Yo*, nowadays, has almost turned into an object of ridicule, being called, for instance, a "commercial travesty and . . . a will-to-power rendition of the Teton Sioux."[22]

This incessant history of white mystification with Indianness just described has anticipated white shamanism of the 1980s and 1990s. From the eighties onwards, white writers have started to disembark from the increasingly risky concept of playing Indian by blood. What they have in mind, nowadays, is paying homage to Indianness, while at the same time ascertaining that their heritage is putatively white. Embodying Indianness by blood, thus, is on a steady decline. Indian grandparents, especially grandmothers, are less fictionalized today as they used to be. However, what could be called 'the Indian granny factor' proves indicative for white shamanic moralizing about Indian heroism. It still happens that American individuals proudly present themselves as offspring of an Indian ancestor. This ancestor, in most cases, is usually referred to as grandparent, favorably a grandmother. This granny, however, is almost always a very dubious character, meaning that her grandchild has never met her in person. Usually, she had died before her spiritual heir (to Indianness, that is) was born. Besides, there exist no records of her life or identity, either. Most documentation has got lost or destroyed, and, unfortunately, this grandmother has also never been able to enroll herself in the lists of the claimed tribe. Another excuse for missing proof of her Indian descent is that she has been ashamed of this cultural heritage. It is exactly this cultural heritage that is mentioned ubiquitously by her grandchild. Another predictable statement about this grandmother is her affiliation to one of the most famous and, thus, favored tribes, for example, Cherokee, Sioux, Cheyenne, or Apache.

Cherokee by far outnumbers any other tribe. Devon A. Mihesuah mentions a list of showbiz people, claiming to be Cherokee (Kim Basinger, Angelina Jolie, and Steven Seagal can also be added to this list): "Even some prominent actors, writers, models and entertainers claim to be part Indian, such as Cher, Val Kilmer, Chuck Norris, Wayne Newton, and Lou Diamond Phillips (all supposedly Cherokees). There is no question that ethnicity is 'in.'"[23] The reasons for the Cherokees' popularity could be predominantly historical ones. During the initial periods of white settlement in Cherokee areas, this tribe was overwhelmingly perceived in a positive light by the pioneers. Judged by white perceptions and standards, their tribal structure seemed most similar to European life at that time. Having their own alphabet – invented by Sequoya – distinguished them even further from the 'other savages' in white eyes, for developing written language was an indicator for the Cherokee tribe becoming civilized. Thus, they were encouraged and supported to become Europeanized in political terms as well. They assimilated easily by owning plantations, keeping slaves, and intermarrying with whites. As they became too successful in their assimilation and, consequently, in the way of European expansion, they got bluntly dispossessed and deported from their main lands in the Southeast. What has become known as the Trail of Tears, is considered tragic and deplorable, even by people otherwise indifferent to Native American issues. This fatal march provided members of this tribe with the status of passive victims, sacrificed for white needs. As contemporary ethnostalgia always glorifies this status of being Indian, it is only natural that most wannabe Indians claim to be part Cherokee.

Until recently, this (Cherokee) brainchild has usually been described as princess. Within this context, Pocahontas – *the* Indian princess – still lingers. She is the prototypical example of the 'good' Indian, embracing civilization and Christianity, while still representing Indian and feminine virtues such as hospitality and obedience.[24] The image of Pocahontas, the princess, the token Indian woman conveys a justifiable and, thus, legitimate impression of monarchy for American history. While otherwise official aristocracy was admonished during the phase of nation building, the figure of Pocahontas got manufactured into an oligarchic godmother of the young American Nation and kept that position ever since. Despite slogans like 'taxation without representation is tyranny,' and a decided antipathy towards monarchy or an explicit aristocratic class, the (young) American Nation found, amongst others, as, for instance, the Kennedy Clan, in Pocahontas something like a royal substitute. Besides, whenever Native Americans and African Americans are set in relation to each other, white perception is still determined by a subtly racist concept of hierarchy, with 'red' ranking somewhat higher than 'black' in this artificial hierarchy.[25]

After the first waves of ethnic enthusiasm, triggered by films like *Dances with Wolves*, had been over, people became more sensitized concerning the term princess. With more and more Native Americans, anthropologists, and historians arguing that there has never been such a concept as 'princess' in Native American cultures, and even TV shows like *Roseanne* making fun of that assumption, wannabes quickly abandoned this term. Geary Hobson, for instance, deconstructs the term princess by opposing it to *squaw*: "[A]lways *Princess*, not merely an Indian *woman* – and certainly *never*, a *squaw*, although they will refer to other Indian women as squaws, but not their own mythical Indian grandmothers."[26] Unlike 'princess,' the term 'squaw' is still widely used, even by 'friends' of the Indian, without being aware of its misogynistic connotation. Squaw, originally, was derogatory for female genitals, with reference to Native American women being considered as sexual objects only. For instance, they would be treated as bargains by trappers or kept as cooks and prostitutes. The increasing discussions about renaming geographical sites like Squaw Peak, for example, might be helpful in bringing about a process of rethinking in using such offensive terminology:

> People who would never speak or write words like "darky" or "mulatto" or "mammy" or "pickaninny" take no notice at all of "red-skin" or "half-breed" or "squaw" or "papoose." So pervasive has been the popular culture and history book misuse that millions of Americans would be stunned to discover that "squaw," for instance, is not a universal word in "Indian" for woman or wife but is instead (say most language experts) a corruption of a regionalism of the Algonquian tonque [*sic*] (dark-horse theory makes squaw a distortion of an Iroquois word denoting female sexual parts). Whatever its origin, the word has been almost universally a white convenience and is scarcely laudatory.[27]

Due to white shamanism, the historical layout of going native by blood, with appertaining Indian forebears, commences to disintegrate for the first time. New Age Indians of white shaman circles explicitly discontinue an ethnic procreation. Instead, they educe a blueprint of Indianness, overwhelmingly characterized by spirit/mind factors. Hence, esotericizing Indianness means 'etiolating' it. Going native, more than ever, happens as a conviction, a life style, a philosophy. Consequently, the white shamanic shift from blood/genes to mind/spirit equalizes neo-primitivism.

One of the first and certainly best-known white shamans, reinventing the neo-noble savage for white shaman purposes, is Lynn V. Andrews. Publishing a series of books, dealing with primitive teachers and medicine people of the most diverse ethnic background – for example, Maori and Aboriginal peoples – Andrews has become somewhat like a role model or godmother for future white shamans. Considering herself, first and foremost, an urbanized shaman, she explicitly focuses on 'her' noble savages' spiritual wisdom. In her 'visionary autobiography' *Medicine Woman*, she tells her heavily challenged life story of becoming the personal trainee to "a Choctaw woman living near a Canadian Cree community in a Pawnee earth lodge, described in such a way as to sound suspiciously like George Catlin's paintings of Mandan Houses from 1832."[28] It is exactly Andrews blending of basically incompatible tribal features that has raised suspicion and contempt. Alice Kehoe provides a good resumé of Andrews' contradicting statements about her alleged Indian encounters:

> There is a town in California called Crowley; there is none by that name in Manitoba. . . . Ruby, and the other Indians on the reserve at "Crowley," call Andrews *wasichu*, the Lakota – not Cree – word for Euroamericans, with spelling following Neihardt's in *Black Elk Speaks*. . . . Why a rural Manitoba woman from a [*sic*] Algonquian Cree community would go through a Siouan ritual, and why these Cree would use a language foreign to them, Andrews never explains. Possibly Ruby and Agnes are really Dakota Sioux, who in fact have several reserves around Brandon, and possibly Andrews has never become aware of the substantial differences between Cree and Sioux?[29]

In addition to the fact that Andrews has probably created a fictional reservation scenario, there arises the legitimate question why – if her story was true – a native woman would resort "not to other Indians, but to a good-hearted white writer to preserve his or her sacred knowledge."[30] Further, Andrews' decision to place Agnes and Ruby on a reserve in Canada is a particularly clever device. Since reservation land is always regarded as the primitive counterpart to the civilized urban environment, it symbolizes the ideal natural surrounding for the white protagonist's catharsis. By choosing a Canadian reserve over a U.S. reservation, Andrews distinguishes this habitat even further from civilization, depicting an island of 'harmonious nature.' This strategy makes her re-create 'the frontier,' which her readers then can overcome metaphorically, reexperiencing what Frederick Turner has called "the luxury of regret."[31] Besides, the political implications of selecting Canadian native territories should not be underestimated. Placing Agnes and Ruby on something like 'neutral' ground – as seen from a U.S. American perspective – enables Andrews to fade out any negative aspects of U.S.-Indian history that might have to be addressed otherwise and, naturally, would counteract the readers' gratification of the story.

Following up on Andrew's writing, which has somehow created a 'white shaman lobby,' there appeared a multitude of authors, availing themselves to Indianness and/or (Indian) shamanism. It would be an extremely ludicrous task to mention this almost endless list of names, that seems to be getting longer by every single day. Amongst the most prominent writers are, for instance, Kenneth Meadows, Brad Steiger, Michael Bromley, and Jamie Sams. Some of these writers explicitly stress the shamanic aspect, while others treat it only marginally. What all writers have in common, however, is their interest in Indianness and Indian spirituality as means of self-discovery, self-recovery, and self-fulfillment.

In his prolific number of books, Kenneth Meadows, for example, emphasizes distinctively on the shamanic path towards healing powers. Underlying this concept, there is the strongly New Agean related idolatry of 'Mother Earth' images. This obvious New Age element earns negative remarks by New Age critics. Thus, responses to Meadows' books are twofold, dealing with his appropriation of either Indianness or New Age philosophies.[32]

Brad Steiger is another writer closely associated with the New Age movement. Steiger is perhaps the best example of how versatile New Agers can be. Being "a part of the mystical counterculture since 1957," he criss-crossed between "trance-channeling, UFOs, UFO-abductions, psychic powers, superadvanced ancient civilizations, crystal magic, Native American and Eastern religions, and so forth."[33] The increasing esoteric Indian mania of the 1990s has made him resort to publishing books about that matter – *Indian Wisdom and Its Guiding Power*

(1991), *American Indian Medicine Dreambook* (1993), *Totems: The Transformative Power of Your Personal Animal Totem* (1997) – abandoning his previous topics like the *Gods of Aquarius*, for example. Steiger's case shows how easily, first of all, New Age writers can hop in between the different fields, secondly, how quickly one can turn into an expert on Indianness if the market calls for it.

Michael Bromley comes closest to what can be called a guru figure in the 1990s. Generally referred to as 'Grandfather Michael,' he gives lectures and holds seminars, basically involving every branch of the general complex New Age. His counseling activities include topics like, for example, *The Search for the Light, Etheric Bodies, Telepathy, Astrology*, and *Karma*. He owns a home page with an Internet Tarot Service, where 'seekers' can e-mail for advice. Despite calling himself a 'Celtic Shaman,' he draws heavily from indigenous cultures all over the world. Bromley sees himself as fighter for primitive people and their rights, always accentuating their spiritual tradition and the utility of this spirituality for the civilized world.

Jamie Sams is a good example of how problematic the question of Native American identity and, thus, authenticity can be. Claiming to be of Seneca/Cherokee descent, Sams is always eager to have herself portrayed in Indian fashion (i.e., long, dark hair and dream catcher accessories). Her name even being registered on one of the lists of enrolled tribal writers in the U.S., Sams particularly utilizes the cliche of the Indian (woman) being close to nature. Undoubtedly writing for a predominantly female clientele, she frequently delineates femininity/fertility and 'Mother Earth' images. The genuineness of her Native American identity is severely questioned by Native Americans themselves. Generally – as verifying authenticity, most of the time, turns into a futile process – it is advisable to look at how writers vanquish an artificial concept of Indianness and construe this concept as a means to rectify their (and their readers) various discontents with civilization.

Most white shaman writings follow a very structured, predictable pattern. The white shaman usually suffers from overcivilization, looking for new ways to ameliorate their overwhelmingly materialistic life. They refer to themselves as 'normal' citizens with common interests, and a particular inclination to socializing and nature loving. Their most favored status is either single (hardly divorced) or family person, either of which is always combined with a strong sense for the so-called community. This emphasized feeling of responsibility for communal life, then, becomes complementary to their wariness about the society they are part of. As they describe themselves as reasonably well situated/educated, they are Mr. And Mrs. Nice Guy from next door. Never too rich, never too smart, they are always eager to present themselves as strictly 'average.' When it comes to the vast bulk of their readers, these facts make their personae easily identifiable with. This, of course, is also true for their stated concern about their society's spiritual and emotional wellbeing. They make their audience share this anxiety about society's growing callousness and its effect on the individual mind. Their verbal pondering about finding themselves through new ways of spiritual awareness is rich in subtle techniques of what can be called a postmodern 'captatio benevolentiae.' The readers are being told what they unconsciously look for in those texts in first place: a hundred percent safe and easy guide through their self-confessed maze of a high-speed, high-tech world.

As white shamans keep a very general tone about themselves, hardly anything about their actual identity is known. Biographical information is rare and, if anything, reduced to a biographical sketch of two or three sentences, usually combined with an 'Indianized' image of the author. For instance, a feather in long, straight, dark hair or a dream wheel around their neck should catch the readers' eye and interest. The author's metamorphosis from average citizen, discontented with civilization, to white shaman, enlightened by spiritual knowledge, is always the same: prior to their change, they used to be moderately successful people with every reason to be happy and satisfied with their lives. However, they could not help but feel spiritually impoverished and disappointed by society's hypocrisy. Failing to become appeased by material wealth, they started to look for ways to fill the growing emotional gap in their lives. They always stress the initial process of this search for their personal holy grail as having been overwhelmingly unconscious (i.e., they looked for something missing in their lives without actually knowing what they were looking for). All of those factors are mentioned to resemble the readers' outright state of mind. Most readers, resorting to white shaman writing to implement their lives, do not necessarily have to be won over. Once they have decided to go for this genre of writing – often referred to as 'visionary autobiography' – they are already compliant with its content, otherwise the mechanism of wishful thinking applied to those texts (i.e., the text should enhance chances in one's own life) would not work. Elements of identification within white shaman books, however, rise their level of dedication, while at the same time minimizing any possible rest of skepticism.

After a certain period of questioning and longing, white shamans, then, always find their spiritual teacher by some sudden, magic incident, which they can never quite fully explain. This spiritual teacher appears in the figure of a mysterious Indian elder, talking mostly in cryptic metaphors. Sometimes, this figure is only the messenger for another, even more enigmatic, even older Indian character, who, accordingly, personifies the 'truest' of all teachers. This deliberate implementation of a certain trinity (i.e., white shaman-teacher-superteacher) preconditions the hierarchical character of the quest. The white shaman, necessarily, has to experience certain stages of spiritual development to, finally, find the 'truth.' It implicates a learning procedure of trial and error, which leaves enough room for readers to cope with personal failure and disappointment, without repudiating the actual writing. Another particular device in that initial phase of the quest is the white shaman's confirmed disbelief of their future teachers, telling them that they are the 'chosen ones.' They elaborately describe their reluctance to accept this assigned role as spiritual genius. By doing so, they introduce a certain element of objectivity, which makes their readers trust their honorable intentions as a spiritual guide.

After having been convinced by their Indian teachers that they are the one and only medium to disseminate Indian spirituality and wisdom, white shamans enter the actual path of shamanism. Their study of shamanism under Indian elders is manifold and picturesque. First, they have to endure a phase of painful apprenticeship to their teachers. Being tested in faith, they are sometimes summoned up critically or offended harshly. Elizabeth Cook-Lynn makes fun of this 'test phase' in her *American Indian Intellectualism and the New Indian Story*:

> He/she spends every summer for twenty years in an Indian reservation community, attends hundreds of powwows, endures the dust and the tedium of these weekend-long or four-day communal marathons, puts up with the insults from those who despise his/her curiosity about their lives. He/she makes his/her home in some faraway city available as a crash pad for traveling Indians, loans money which he/she never expects to have returned, lends a car, baby-sits, takes on the responsibility of an "adopted" relative, is thrilled to be given an Indian name which is said to be invested with a mysterious spirituality.[34]

Naturally, the shaman apprentices gain approval as they gain wisdom and soon shed their yoke of being harassed by their masters. They quickly move up the ladder of shamanism, dazzled by the discovery of their special gift for healing and teaching, which the elders have told them about in the first place. They are usually urged by their now generous teachers to pursue this talent and share it with the rest of mankind. The message is a salvation-like one: white shamans should endeavor to help the 'ignorant' overcome the obstacles of civilization. Which, of course, is a very euphemistic way of explaining their reasons for writing those books. They make the Indian teacher responsible for their impulse to produce these texts. Naturally, no one would ever admit that they produce these texts for the mere reason of earning a lot of money (this would go against their shamanic ethics!) As they also invent terms like 'visionary autobiography' for their genre of writing, they choose a clever disguise, which makes it impossible for readers and critics to distinguish between what is real and what is invented. This provides them with a certain form of immunity to actual criticism plus enables them to justify their writing against accusations of being nothing more than preconstructed, fantastic stories in the tradition of Carlos Castaneda.

Any white shaman story about the search for their 'true' inner being incorporates more or less rudimentary forms of symbolism. For their process of spiritual maturity, white shamans usually retreat to a reservation, the geographic setting of which, for obvious reasons, is only vaguely defined. The Indians they get to know there are equally untraceable, displaying a motley mixture of several incompatible tribal features and languages. This display of commonly known tribes enables readers to grab on to their archetypal, for socially conditioned, image of the 'real' Indian. Since "the American Indian in the world consciousness is a treasured invention, a gothic artifact,"[35] white shamanic readers can wallow in a pleasant feeling of anthropological expertise. The topography of the rez meets a crucial purpose in white shaman writing: it is the natural (i.e., primitive) counterpart to the urban (i.e., civilized) setting. Consequently, technology is scarce on the rez. Never is there mentioned a microwave or personal computer, there is not the slightest sign of stress or hectic times in people's lives. Instead, they are in touch with basically untouched nature. The rez is not merely idealized, but turns into a natural island amidst the vast sea of a cultural world.

The zenith of any of these stories about becoming a white shaman is the moment of investigating one's visionary powers. This vision quest, then, develops into a zealous journey. It is particularly in the obligatory vision quest, where the solipsistic character of white shaman writing is most evident – with white shamans falling especially prey to their antediluvian ideas. Everything in the text evolves around the pivotal element of epiphany. After having experienced unique cosmic revelation and, thus, having gained their teachers' final approval, white shamans are ceremoniously renamed. This naming ceremony usually goes along with being adopted as an equal member by the tribe and, therefore, enjoying all the privileges that the white shaman has worked so hard for. In the description of the renaming and adopting ceremony, initiation rituals and (re)birth symbolisms of several cultures are heavily plagiarized. This technique, again, strikes the 'archetypal cord' in readers. The literary device of using familiar symbolism makes readers bond unconsciously with the author. The result is a clientele of readers, who believe that what has happened on this faraway rez is not only true, but can come true for them, too. Thus, such visionary autobiographies become adult fairy tales, with readers reliving white shaman adventures, comparable to children reexperiencing fantastic stories as real. The rez, then, turns into a Land of Oz, the white shaman becomes the Wizard, guiding their readers to their balanced Self.

Thereby, the focus is always on white shamans', not on their teachers' capability to become mediums for this spirituality to the outer world. This discrepancy of Indians staying passive and mute, when it comes to teaching their primitive cultural heritage to civilization, and having whites assume the active role as a public organ instead, is a tragically logic one. It follows the tradition of the simple-minded, illiterate native, being spoken for by the white, sophisticated protector. This reversal of roles (i.e., the white shaman first being apprentice, now being master) is easily acknowledged and accepted by their readership, for Indians are not generally considered to have a voice of their own. While undergoing their shamanic teachings, white shamans have not only become equal in wisdom and prophetic knowledge to their Indian elders. In fact, they have turned out to exceed them, the Indian culture now being even more manifest in their persona than in actual Native American peoples. Their ability to decode Indian culture for vision-hungry whites makes flesh-and-blood Native Americans – and, as a further consequence, a realistic confrontation with their lives – superfluous. This convenient model allows readers to safely play Indian by their own rules and, again, stigmatize Native Americans as the vanishing race. What remains is the memento of a putatively extinct people, which is not troublesome, for there is white shamans to safeguard and carry on their traditions, customs, and teachings.

Any discussion of white shamanism would be incomplete without referring to what has become known as the group of *Plastic Medicine Men*. Plastic Medicine Men pursue similar intentions as white shaman writers by slightly different means. Also beckoned by Indianness and its healing impact on the civilized mind, they offer vision quests, workshops, weekend seminars, and sweat lodges for paying customers. Such camps for pop Indian spirituality are generally widespread in the United States, but particularly concentrated in the West. Native and non-native critics have provided these medicine men and women with the label 'plastic' to express their abomination for the financial plagiarizing of Native American customs, ceremonies, and rituals. Critics' attacks of skepticism about the sellout of native lives by New Age Indianness are equally aimed at Caucasian as well as Native American workshop conductors, who employ Indian artifice. Indeed, medicine (wo)men propagating Indian shamanic healing have been unmasked to emanate from white and Native American communities – the latter, however, would always discredit and invalidate these teachings as inauthentic to tribal accounts.

The best-known medicine man, expelled from Native American circles, is Sun Bear. Sun Bear, claiming to be Chippewa, pioneered the plastic medicine circles by founding his 'own' tribe – the so-called *Bear Tribe* – as early as the beginning of the 1980s. Having worked in various professions before that, including real estate and Hollywood's movie industry, Sun Bear is being denied any official membership of the White Earth Reservation in Minnesota, which he considers his native tribe. His *Bear Tribe*, which consists overwhelmingly of 'Indianized' disciples, is equally dispossessed of authenticity on accredited tribal lists or in tribal records. Hyemeyohsts Storm, author of the highly disapproved *Seven Arrows*, is closely associated with the teachings of the Bear Tribe Medicine Society. Workshops offered by this society mostly revolve around Sun Bear's prolific books about 'the Great Spirit' and 'Mother Earth' and Storm's esoteric modification of the Cheyenne Medicine Wheel in *Seven Arrows*. Storm's identity remains enigmatic – for Michael Castro, for example, there is no doubt that he is non-native[36] – just like his role in the *Deer Tribe*, another society offering sweat/earth lodges. This *Deer Tribe* is organized by a certain Harley Swift Deer Reagan, who is accused of being a bogus Indian by several Native American communities.

Along with Harley Swift Deer Reagan and Rolling Thunder – another notorious medicine man insisting to be Shoshone – there would appear a number of shamanic teachers and healers in the 1980s, whose native pretext is genuinely unsubstantiated. Their premise about Indianness as a substratum for any form of seminars about body, mind, and spirit has become successfully perpetuated and even fortified in the 1990s – the only difference being that the number and variety of workshops and sweat lodges in bucolic surroundings have increased astronomically.

Particularly the Internet turned out to be a precocious medium for Plastic Medicine (Wo)Men. It has turned into a bedrock for promoting and advertising their skills, philosophies, and products. Plastic Medicine (Wo)Men's homepages, naturally, are especially redolent of crash courses in Indian mimesis. This forum for Indian novelties and spiritual counseling is an increasingly important chance for Plastic Medicine (Wo)Men (and, of course, white shamans) to reach esoteric seekers on a global scale.

Thereby, the proclamation of any 'true' Indian stratagem has turned into a secondary issue. A particularly famous group – when it comes to moderating its indigenous influence while perspicuously invigorating vision quests and sweat lodges – is the so-called *Great Round*, headed by Sedonia Cahill and Bird Brother. Mimicking Indian ways plus effacing native origins might seem incompatible and counterproductive at first glance, however, it is prototypical for 'core shamanism,' in which Cahill and Bird Brother participate. What shines through is their desire to invent and create Indian customs, rituals, or prayers rather then taking them over from Native American culture in the first place. These ideas coincide nicely with the general New Age attitude towards Indianness as a means to reinvent oneself and civilized life. The method of making up ceremonies instead of keeping to indelible tribal patterns has already been practiced by the Bear Tribe's Dream Wheel Gatherings. It is a particular strategy to serve the customers' wish to realize Indianness as they please. Instead of sticking to one mandatory tribe, New Age Indians can be particularly eclectic in swerving in between totally different and differing tribes. The individual innovation of ritual, again, provides the feeling of being creative. Both components (i.e., intertribalism and mythopoeia) are crucial for the New Age variant of going native. It evinces a particularly narcissistic nature – narcissism being often called the most characteristic feature of New Agers – as well as the New Age preoccupation with indigenous cultures in general and Native Americans in particular: anyone can become native by any means, the implication being that a realistic, political, or day-to-day interlocution with native people and/or issues is not necessary.

A crucial element in the white shamans' approach to Indians is the method of abstracting the alien Other. This abstraction, sometimes bona fide, sometimes histrionic, reverts severely to one particular aspect in the tradition of white chivalry to Indianness: the fetishistic nature. In his essay *The Noble Savage: Theme As Fetish*, Hayden White analyzes the literary appropriation of the noble savage figure in terms of fetishistic attributes. Though dealing with literature of the 18th and particularly the 19th century, White's model of the noble savage as fetish for white society is essential for comprehending the success of white shamans in the last two decades of the 20th century. Having the opportunity to rely on a massive reservoir of literary material, which deals with the notion of the noble savage, white shamans can be very eclectic in duplicating ideas and implicitly modifying them for their own writing. This procedure involves the vital component of noble savage fetishism as being "at one and the same time, a kind of belief, a kind of devotion, and a kind of psychological set or posture"[37] – a definition, being extracted from an analysis of the ethnological and psychological meaning of the term.

The cultural archeology of white shamanism conduces postmodern retribalizations. As Indianness, for white shamans, is germinated through a state of mind, the cultural bias of it becomes synthesized. The artificial 'cloning' of tribes, for instance, is a common subject in white shaman studies. Lynn V. Andrews, again, pioneered in this area by syndicating her 'global sisterhoods.' White shaman sensationalism about manufacturing Indian personalities/tribes proliferates much more than a mere self-opinionated perception of cultures. Actually, it redirects the most basic cultural intervals. The outcome, unsurprisingly, resembles the end of *Dances with Wolves*. – Whites become codified Indian (in mind), while Indians are, once more, reactivated as the vanishing race. This cultural codex implies a fatalistic occupation of the 'final frontier': ultimately usurping the Other by invading the Other's cultural and mental space.

Incidentally, putative Native American voices are still considered a curio by the general public. Particularly Native American writers experience society's treatment of themselves and their work as hypocritical. They, like any other Native American artist, are not so much judged by their writing, but only bound to their ethnicity. Elizabeth Cook-Lynn, for example, sarcastically complains about the fact that publishers are more interested in her 'heritage' than her actual writing, because "'the American Indian intellectual' is to many people a bizarre phrase, falling quaintly on the unaccustomed ears of those in the American mainstream."[38] Most of all, writers are regarded as artifacts and, thus, placed in a history showcase, their works frequently appearing along the shelves of the 'anthropology' section of bookstores, while white shamans' books can be found along the 'Native American Studies' shelves. Accordingly, the selections of works in bookshops mirror those in private homes of people showing an interest in Indianness: white shaman books by far outnumber Native American writing, which is usually merely represented by a copy of *Ceremony*. Writers like Silko or Momaday, then, turn into "a kind of cultural hybrid, or cultural half-caste,"[39] since the mainstream reading public assumes them to forfeit 'true' Indianness. Thus, white shamans often replace authentic Native American writers in the eyes of this reading public, because they deprive Native American authors of some of the most powerful forums to express their culture and cultural problems. White shaman writers produce convenient texts about cliches, which readers do not have to question, whereas most genuine Native American authors demand a by far greater critical reflection on Indianness, white history, culture, or politics. As their writing leaves hardly any room for complacency *or* pity, it is a much more challenging literature than most readers want to deal with. Additionally, the economic boom of white shaman literature seems to be impetuous. 'Shaman,' in general, has become a very frequent term to occur in titles of particularly self-help or D-I-Y-books.[40] Success appears to be programmed whenever 'shaman' decorates the book cover, while white shamans per se adopt this term beyond decoration. Their fancy combination of shamanism and Indianness, peppered with neo-noble savage images, discredits Native American literary, political, and social polyvocality.

Naturally, white shamanic egotism sparks critical responses from Native American communities. Parallel to white shamans, producing masses of texts that stereotype Indianness, Native Americans implement critiques of these New Age Indians by deconstructing stereotypical features. Most of the time, they choose a jocular tone, ridiculing wannabe Indians irreverently. At the same time, however, they make clear, how onerous it seems to fight against the bastions of stereotypical images over and over again. Leslie Marmon Silko has been one of the first writers to zero in on impostors of Native American poetry. In her *Old-Time Indian Attack*, she accuses poets, relying on the "universal consciousness"[41] to portray Indian mentality, of stealing cultural property. Silko is joined in her attack by Wendy Rose, expressing her contempt with wannabe Indians both through prose as well as poetry. For instance, her poem *For the White Poets Who Would Be Indian*, aims at unmasking white shamans' superficial culture hopping.[42]

Gerald Vizenor, again, is particularly concerned with white *invention* of Indian figures. By using irony as effective tool, Vizenor frequently introduces trickster elements in his writing. The indomitable nature of white shaman tribalism plagiarizes this image of the invented Indian a fortiori. Most prevalently, the automatism of this image displays not merely inventions, but also – as Michael Dorris has noted – *ignorance*.[43] Deduced by white shamanism, Indianness, however, experiences another changeover. By outranking nativism, white shamans revert invention and ignorance to *identity*. What white shamanism strives for is an Indianness sui generis. The soigné stepping stone for this pursuit is New Age rhetoric. The succeeding chapter, thus, is designed to dissect esotericism as circumstantial artistry for white shamanism.

Notes

1. Leah Dilworth, *Imagining Indians in the Southwest: Persistent Visions of a Primitive Past* (Washington, D.C., and London: Smithsonian Institution Press, 1996), 209.

2. Cf. Ruth Benedict, *Patterns of Culture* (Boston: Houghton Mifflin, 1989), chap. 6.

3. Mircea Eliade, *Shamanism: Archaic Techniques of Ecstasy*, trans. Willard R. Trask (Paris: Librairie Payot, 1951; Princeton: Princeton University Press, 1974), 4.

4. Peter Farb, *Man's Rise to Civilization As Shown by the Indians of North America from Primeval Times to the Coming of the Industrial State* (New York: E. P. Dutton, 1968), 50.

5. For an analysis of the concept of 'the raped soul,' see Forrest E. Clements, *Primitive Concepts of Disease* (Berkeley: n.p., 1932).

6. Geary Hobson, "The Rise of the White Shaman As a New Version of Cultural Imperialism," in *The Remembered Earth: An Anthology of Contemporary Native American Literature*, ed. Geary Hobson (n.p.: Red Earth Press, 1979; Albuquerque: University of New Mexico Press, 1991), 102.

7. Robert F Berkhofer Jr., Commentary to *Indian-White Relations: A Persistent Paradox*, eds. Jane F. Smith and Robert M. Kvasnicka (Washington, D.C.: Howard University Press, 1976), 84.

8. Mary Louise Pratt, *Imperial Eyes: Travel Writing and Transculturation* (London and New York: Routledge, 1992), 7.

9. For a discussion of the difficulties, involved with bilateral collaboration on oral literature, see Arnold Krupat, "An Approach to Native American Texts," in *Critical Essays on Native American Literature*, ed. Andrew Wiget (Boston: G. K. Hall, 1985), 116-31.

The problem of the white outsider, who intrudes upon a native community, trying to gather 'original' anthropological material from their 'informants,' is a general one, well known at least since Margaret Mead's *Coming of Age in Samoa*. For reevaluations of anthropological contact zones, see Marianna Torgovnick, *Gone Primitive: Savage Intellects, Modern Lives* (Chicago and London: University of Chicago Press, 1990) and, contrastingly, Marjorie Perloff, "Tolerance and Taboo: *Modernist Primitives and Postmodernist Pieties*," in *Prehistories of the Future: The Primitivist Project and the Culture of Modernism*, ed. Elazar Barkan and Ronald Bush (Stanford: Stanford University Press, 1995), 339-54.

10. People calling themselves 'Indian friend' are usually very fond of having been adopted by a particular tribe. A good example for this is Leslie A. Fiedler, acknowledging credits to the Blackfoot Tribe. Cf. Leslie A. Fiedler, *The Return of the Vanishing American* (New York: Stein and Day Publishers, 1968), iii. This acknowledgment is implicitly mocked by Robert Baird. Cf. Robert Baird, "'Going Indian': *Dances with Wolves* (1990)," in *Hollywood's Indian: The Portrayal of the Native American in Film*, eds. Peter C. Rollins and John E. O'Connor (Lexington: University Press of Kentucky, 1998), 153.

11. In his novel *Indian Killer*, for example, Sherman Alexie has his female protagonist Marie sarcastically comment on this autobiography. Cf. Sherman Alexie, *Indian Killer* (New York: Warner Books, 1998), 58.

12. Elizabeth Cook-Lynn, "American Indian Intellectualism and the New Indian Story," in *Natives and Academics: Researching and Writing about American Indians*, ed. Devon A. Mihesuah (Lincoln and London: University of Nebraska Press, 1998), 120.

13. For a written documentary of this phenomenon, with particular emphasis on writers like Mary Austin, Mabel Dodge Luhan, and D. H. Lawrence, see Arrell Morgan Gibson, *The Santa Fe and Taos Colonies: Age of the Muses, 1900-1942* (Norman: University of Oklahoma Press, 1983).

14. For an analysis of the congruence between power lines of literacy and discrimination, see Paul Gunn Allen, *Off the Reservation: Reflections on Boundary-Busting, Border-Crossing, Loose Canons* (Boston: Beacon Press, 1998), chap. 1.

15. Gaile McGregor, *The Noble Savage in the New World Garden: Notes towards a Syntactics of Place* (Bowling Green, Ohio: Bowling Green State University Popular Press, 1988), 216.

16. Cf. Vine Deloria Jr., ed., *Frank Waters: Man and Mystic* (Athens: Swallow Press/Ohio University Press, 1993).

17. Elémire Zolla, *The Writer and the Shaman: A Morphology of the American Indian*, trans. Raymond Rosenthal (n.p.: Casa Editrice Valentino Bompiani, 1969; New York: Harcourt Brace Jovanovich, 1973), 222.

18. Cf. Michael Dorris, "Native American Literature in an Ethnohistorical Context," in *Paper Trail: Essays* (New York: HarperPerennial, 1994), 243.

19. Vine Deloria Jr., *God Is Red: A Native View of Religion* (Golden, CO: Fulcrum Publishing, 1993), 26.

20. David Murray, *Modern Indians: Native Americans in the Twentieth Century*; BAAS Pamphlets in American Studies 8 (Durham and Long Beach, CA: BAAS, 1982), 36.

21. Richard de Mille, "Validity Is Not Authenticity: Distinguishing Two Components of Truth," in *The Invented Indian: Cultural Fictions and Government Policies*, ed. James A. Clifton (New Brunswick, NJ, and London: Transaction Publishers, 1996), 252.

22. Kenneth Lincoln, *Native American Renaissance* (Berkeley, Los Angeles, and London: University of California Press, 1983), 31.

23. Devon A. Mihesuah, *American Indians: Stereotypes and Realities* (Atlanta and Regina: Clarity Press, 1998), 100.

24. For research on mythopoeia of the Pocahontas figure, see Christian F. Feest, "Pride and Prejudice: The Pocahontas Myth and the Pamunkey," in *The Invented Indian: Cultural Fictions and Government Policies*, ed. James A. Clifton (New Brunswick, NJ, and London: Transaction Publishers, 1996), 49-61, Charles R. Larson *American Indian Fiction* (Albuquerque: University of New Mexico Press, 1979), chap. 2, and Klaus Theweleit, *Pocahontas in Wonderland: Shakespeare on Tour*, vol. 1 (Frankfurt am Main and Basel: Stroemfeld/Roter Stern, 1999).

For studies on Pocahontas symbolism on stage and in movies, see Pauline Turner Strong, "Playing Indian in the Nineties: *Pocahontas* and *The Indian in the Cupboard*," in *Hollywood's Indian: The Portrayal of the Native American in Film*, eds. Peter C. Rollins and John E. O'Connor (Lexington: University of Kentucky Press, 1998), 187-205, and Susan Scheckel, *The Insistence of the Indian: Race and Nationalism in Nineteenth-Century American Culture* (Princeton: Princeton University Press, 1998), chap. 3.

25. For analyses of reconceptualizations of the Aristotelian view and skin color racism, see Henri Baudet, *Paradise on Earth: Some Thoughts on European Images of Non-European Man*, trans. Elizabeth Wentholt (n.p.: Royal Van Gorcum, 1959; New Haven and London: Yale University Press, 1965), Hugh Honour, *The European Vision of America* (Cleveland, Ohio: Cleveland Museum of Art, 1975), and Joel W. Martin, "'My Grandmother Was a Cherokee Princess': Representations of Indians in Southern History," in *Dressing in Feathers: The Construction of the Indian in American Popular Culture*, ed. S. Elizabeth Bird (Boulder, CO, and Oxford: Westview Press, 1998), 129-47.

26. Geary Hobson, "The Rise of the White Shaman As a New Version of Cultural Imperialism," in *The Remembered Earth: An Anthology of Contemporary Native American Literature*, ed. Geary Hobson (n.p.: Red Earth Press, 1979; Albuquerque: University of New Mexico Press, 1991), 100; Hobson's emphasis.

27. Raymond William Stedman, *Shadows of the Indian: Stereotypes in American Culture* (Norman: University of Oklahoma Press, 1982), 241.

28. Philip J. Deloria, *Playing Indian* (New Haven and London: Yale University Press, 1998), 174.

29. Alice Kehoe, "Primal Gaia: Primitivists and Plastic Medicine Men," in *The Invented Indian: Cultural Fictions and Government Policies*, ed. James A. Clifton (New Brunswick, NJ, and London: Transaction Publishers, 1996), 204. It is important to mention, however, that Kehoe – next to Feest, Clifton, Tooker, Gill, de Mille, and Feraca in *The Invented Indian* – is in turn criticized by Vine Deloria Jr. for equally appropriating Indianness on scholarly grounds. Cf. Vine Deloria Jr., "Comfortable Fictions and the Struggle for Turf: An Essay Review of *The Invented Indian: Cultural Fictions and Government Policies*," in *Natives and Academics: Researching and Writing about American Indians*, ed. Devon A. Mihesuah (Lincoln and London: University of Nebraska Press, 1998), 65-83.

30. Philip J. Deloria, *Playing Indian* (New Haven and London: Yale University Press, 1998), 174.

31. Frederick Turner, *Beyond Geography: The Western Spirit against the Wilderness* (New York: Viking Press, 1980), 16.

32. For a discussion of Meadows' New Agean affiliations, see M. D. Faber, *New Age Thinking: A Psychoanalytic Critique* (Ottawa: University of Ottawa Press, 1996), part 2.

33. Robert Basil, "'A Vast Spiritual Kindergarten': Talking with Brad Steiger," in *Not Necessarily the New Age: Critical Essays*, ed. Robert Basil (Buffalo, NY: Prometheus Books, 1988), 226.

34. Elizabeth Cook-Lynn, "American Indian Intellectualism and the New Indian Story," in *Natives and Academics: Researching and Writing about American Indians*, ed. Devon A. Mihesuah (Lincoln and London: University of Nebraska Press, 1998), 122-23.

35. Louis Owens, *Other Destinies: Understanding the American Indian Novel* (Norman and London: University of Oklahoma Press, 1992), 4.

36. Cf. Michael Castro, *Interpreting the Indian: Twentieth-Century Poets and the Native American* (Albuquerque: University of New Mexico Press, 1983; Norman and London: University of Oklahoma Press, 1991), 155.

37. Hayden White, "The Noble Savage: Theme As Fetish," in *First Images of America: The Impact of the New World on the Old*, ed. Fredi Chiappelli (Berkeley, Los Angeles, and London: University of California Press, 1976), 1: 122.

38. Elizabeth Cook-Lynn, "American Indian Intellectualism and the New Indian Story," in *Natives and Academics: Researching and Writing about American Indians*, ed. Devon A. Mihesuah (Lincoln and London: University of Nebraska Press, 1998), 111.

39. Charles R. Larson *American Indian Fiction* (Albuquerque: University of New Mexico Press, 1979), 166.

40. For a book on creative writing, incorporating the term 'shaman,' see, for example, Robert Burdette Sweet, *Writing towards Wisdom: The Writer As Shaman* (St. Louis, MO: Helios House, 1990).

41. Leslie Marmon Silko, "An Old-Time Indian Attack Conducted in Two Parts: Part One : Imitation 'Indian' Poems, Part Two: Gary Snyder's Turtle Island," in *The Remembered Earth: An Anthology of Contemporary Native American Literature*, ed. Geary Hobson (n.p.: Red Earth Press, 1979; Albuquerque: University of New Mexico Press, 1991), 212.

42. Cf. Wendy Rose, "For the White Poets Who Would Be Indian," in *The Third Woman: Minority Women Writers of the United States*, ed. Dexter Fisher (Boston: Houghton Mifflin, 1980), 86-87.

43. Cf. Michael Dorris, "'I' Isn't for 'Indian,'" in *Paper Trail: Essays* (New York: HarperPerennial, 1994), 120-21.

2. New Age Goes Native

As the end of the millennium approaches, the New Age seems to be everywhere but continues to elude specific definition.
Marianna Torgovnick, *Primitive Passions: Men, Women, and the Quest for Ecstasy*

New Age bookstores are chock-a-block with spiritualizing treatises on supposed traditional native beliefs, while gurus urge repressed modern males to flee to the woods, to become "real" men by howling and drumming, by becoming "warriors." By acting "like Indians," it would seem, we may become noble, free, authentic: we may discover our true selves.
Fergus M. Bordewich, *Killing the White Man's Indian: Reinventing Native Americans at the End of the Twentieth Century*

White shamanistic adaptability shows particularly in its cultivation of New Agean attitudes, managing an almost seamless fusion of esotericism and Indianness. A brief historic inquiry about what is generally known as 'The New Age Movement' at the beginning of this chapter will expose the cryptic character of this movement. Opacity of anything New Agean when it is meant to pin-point ideologies or definitions, for example, provides the ideal culture medium for white shamanism. Ergo, the blossoming of countless New Age branches in the 1980s also anticipated future white shamanic claimants to Indianness. New Agean forms of neo-paganism or neo-animism, for instance, evinced antecedent transgressions to Indianness.

What started off as New Age in the 1960s and 1970s (particularly in the United States and Great Britain), was – even at that time – a relatively amorphous construct of various teachings, utilizing a wide range of aspects from such different fields as parapsychology or Asian religions, for example. Towards the end of the 1980s, it gradually dissolved into an iridescent spectrum of more or less loosely interconnected disciplines, which are not explicitly labeled New Age any longer. Marianna Torgovnick, analyzing New Age and New Agean affiliated tendencies in *Primitive Passions*, captured this iridescence:

> It [the New Age] includes phenomena as diverse as Yoga and the Kabbalah, holistic healing and Wicca, veganism and acupuncture, contact with angels and spiritual computer interfaces, wilderness trips and tours of holy places, self-help and Jungian psychology, goddess revivals, and even the mythopoetic men's movement . . . It is a decidedly eclectic collection of phenomena, drawing from a variety of cultural and religious traditions, past and present, Western and Eastern, modern and primitive, familiar and exotically Other.[1]

Due to negative connotations, which the original term New Age has acquired over the years, it is nowadays much safer for authors and publishers alike to resort to new expressions such as *self-help*, *self-improvement*, *natural living*, *inner healing*, or *new science*. Thus, a direct link of several groupings, dealing with esoteric and/or metaphysical material, to the former New Age is not evident in most cases. By hinting at Gallup Poll statistics, for instance, James R Lewis demonstrates how thoroughly integrated mystic ideas are in everyday life of average U.S. citizens. As also pointed out by James R. Lewis, the statistical figures reveal no discrepancy in combining religious beliefs of traditional churches with unorthodox ideologies:

> One also needs to take account of the many people who consciously avoid being associated with the New Age. In contrast to the media stereotype of the colorful New Ager who walks around in conspicuous crystal jewelry while spouting incoherent New Age philosophy, most movement participants tend to keep a low profile with respect to their religious beliefs and practices. . . . The presence of large numbers of movement participants at elite levels of society is thus not immediately evident to the casual observer.[2]

The New Age movement has never been a homogenous one. Accordingly, a historical retrospective of the origin and evolution of New Age is difficult and problematic. Difficult, for almost every historical analysis of New Age tendencies presents a different time scale with varying key figures; problematic, for almost any writing on New Age cannot help but be emotional in one way or the other. The polarity of pro- and con-New Age writers annihilates any possible objective perspective on the subject. The prolific number of academic and nonacademic disputes is characterized by subtle forms of criticism as well as open hostility. Since it is almost exclusively religious scholars and New Agers dealing with this subject, these disputes are characterized by extreme, sometimes radical, views. Constance Cumbey's *The Hidden Dangers of the Rainbow* (1983) is perhaps the best example for a very fanatic (almost paranoid) form of con-New Age writing, heavily criticizing, amongst others, David Spangler, for instance. Spangler, on the other hand, contributed to a pro-New Age book, edited by Duncan S. Ferguson, *New Age Spirituality: An Assessment* (1993). This book is exemplary for most pro-New Age compilations, since the 'pro' is cleverly disguised. The writers' true attitudes and intentions do not show openly. Instead, they assume an allegedly neutral, (pseudo)scientific point of view. Nevertheless, any of these 'analyses' is implicitly arguing for New Age movements.

Nowhere else is this fatal binary opposition better demonstrated than through responses to Fritjof Capra's writing. A trained physicist, Capra has produced predominantly metaphysical books, and, accordingly, has been criticized or praised for it. Whereas James R. Lewis calls Capra's work an attempt "to reconcile science and mysticism,"[3] Henry Gordon finds more drastic words for Capra's *The Tao of Physics* (1983), claiming it to be "a murky hodge-podge of pseudoscientific theories sure to influence the unsophisticated student."[4] M. D. Faber, again, juxtaposes *The Tao* with psychoanalysis:

> Let us say for the sake of argument that the universe *is* some sort of giant hologram; let us say that every particle, or wave, *is* related in some vibratory fashion to every other particle or wave; let us say that all things *are* "interconnected," that everything *is* "woven" together at the dynamic level of the cosmic "web." The question arises immediately from the psychoanalytic standpoint, *so what*? Are these assumptive physical factors supposed to cancel out, or diminish, or modify, even for one moment, the emotional, psychic realities of our developmental lives? Do New Agers actually believe that appreciation of such "cosmic" properties, such "dancing wu li" physical features, will alter, even for one moment,

the tenor of our unconscious minds as those minds have been shaped in and through the internalizations of the past? Such assumptive, speculative factors, even if we believe them wholeheartedly, are but straws in the psychic wind of our actual, character-producing experience.[5]

Once the obstacle of gathering comparatively neutral background information is overcome, the problem of evaluating historical studies in terms of chronology has to be faced. All scholars agree on the fact that the New Age movement emerging in the last three decades of the 20th century is not really 'new.' However, when it comes to determining the actual historic beginnings of this movement, agreement ceases to exist. Some like, for example, religious studies scholar Robert Ellwood go as far as to Hellenism and Neoplatonism[6] to find the most ancient roots of New Age. Others like, for instance, Kay Alexander[7] consider Swedenborgianism and Mesmerism as crucial schools of thought for the development of New Agean beliefs. The foundation of the Theosophical Society by Madame Helena Blavatsky and Henry Steele Olcott 1875 in New York, however, is collectively mentioned as the starting point for the (post)modern New Age. One of the Society's members, Alice Bailey, is credited for 'inventing' the term New Age. After having been expelled from the Blavatsky group, Bailey formed the Arcane School in 1923 and started to write a series of books. Among such flamboyant titles like, for instance, *The Externalization of the Hierarchy, Initiation,* or *Human and Solar,* there can also be found *Education in the New Age.* Marilyn Ferguson is responsible for another pivotal book, *The Aquarian Conspiracy* (1980), which is generally considered the most significant one at the dawn of the contemporary New Age wave.

Particularly the 1960s and the hippie era paved the way for gurus of any kind. Thus, New Age turned from a once marginal into a mainstream phenomenon, displaying the most multiple facets. "Past lives therapists and crystal healers, earth goddesses and lost civilizations, mantras and gurus, Harmonic Convergence and shamanic voyages, Hollywood ghosts and California channelers,"[8] are only but a few examples of how multilayered New Age can be. This is also true for the different labels and terms applied to New Age or diverse New Age related groups. Amongst the most commonly used attributes are, for instance, wicca, transcendental, and neo-pagan. The term neo-paganism is particularly interesting, because it signifies a new tendency within the New Age matrix. For Michael York, the seamless fusion between New Agers and neo-pagans happens through animism and shamanism:

> The strongest areas of overlap between Neo-paganism and New Age lie in the Earth Religions, Native American Spirituality, and Shamanism. . . . An underlying element behind New Age teachings/practices concerning Earth Religions/Native American Practices/Shamanism is the animistic perception that sees all things as imbued with an inherent vitality.[9]

At the end of the 1980s, there appeared a general interest in indigenous cultures, ancient rituals, and primitive customs, which has not lost its fascination for the several esoteric communities ever since. On the contrary, neo-paganism found a profitable niche in what Henry Gordon called "the occult market."[10] Henceforth, there has been a remarkable shift towards neo-primitivism, and the popularity of shamanic teachers and healers skyrocketed. What is generally referred to as Indian shamanism/spirituality, experienced a definite rush of disciples, too. Thus, esoteric Indianness, as appropriated by white shamans of the 1990s, is one of the many millennialist outgrowths of the New Age movement. At first glance, however, it might seem a bit alienated from the actual New Age by applying labels and techniques in a much more subtle way, so that potential customers would not be scared away by the nowadays almost notorious term New Age.

New Age and white shamanism are complementary when it comes to issues like *diversity*, *diplomacy*, and *domestication*. Esoteric as well as white shamanistic strategies of diversity circulate an industry of wisdom and self-help. To ensure flexibility of choice, attitudes are on an exhaustive display. This self-service store of attitudes, then, enables New Agean/white shamanic customers to dispose to topics of their liking. Therefore, the carving of prolific niches of beliefs makes esoteric/shaman followers arrogate specific topics to themselves, while at the same time effectively fending off other topics. For example, a believer in astrology can go esoteric/native without affiliating themselves to practices they distrust like, for instance, channeling. This wayward diversity, naturally, works for white shamans and esoteric teachers, too, especially when their patented niche of beliefs is threatened to become besmirched by critics. Diversity, then, is either an excuse to feel immune to this criticism, or it can turn into a means to defy this criticism by redirecting it to another niche. A favored comment to meet critique of their work goes something like this: 'We're the wrong ones to be addressed with these accusations. They should be aimed at the black sheep in the movement.' Staying enigmatic is part of New Age/white shaman diplomacy. Beliefs are sold palliatively. So, religiously colored beliefs become trimmed to serve the mainstream public. The so-called domestication of religious beliefs of everyday life offers a loophole for the esoteric market. The smorgasbord of religions, however, is sold unobtrusively, since customers favor a synthesis of 'old' and 'new' religions. Besides, religious esotericism, especially in the 1990s, became adjacent to millennialist aspects. The accumulating apocalyptic, eschatological, and utopian visions concerning the 21st century proved and still prove to be the driving elements for the booming "religioscientific consumerism."[11]

Yet, there is an obvious discrepancy between New Agean professional and ideological representations. Ideally, New Agers want to see themselves as antimaterialist offspring of the sixties' counterculture. Actually, New Age stands for megabusiness, including the creation of trends as well as the production and marketing of trend-ridden items. This sales policy, naturally, results in million dollar profits, which are not always easy to pinpoint for outsiders. In *Understanding the New Age*, Russell Chandler tries to give a critical account of New Age finances. Normally, such 'price lists' are not easily provided. As Chandler also makes explicit, New Age decidedly wants to appear as spiritual movement with no signs of late capitalism attached to it whatsoever. Accordingly, it is equally difficult to access statistics on sales figures of white shaman books. Even authors who propagate "the crossover from spiritualism to materialism"[12] like, for example, Lynn V. Andrews, are hard to come by as an actual 'market factor.' However, considering the enormous amounts of white shaman books being produced every year, the profits can safely be placed within the multimillion dollar scale. Some numbers might help to visualize the gigantic sums already involved in the 1980s: Weekend seminars were placed within the $300, an hour counseling from channeled beings within the $10-300 range. Tapes cost about $11, wired pyramids, a bestseller in the 1980s, $20-120. The money spent on crystals, another favorite New Age element of the 1980s and now reinvented as so-called power beads, was $100 million per year, estimated to hit the $250 million limit at the beginning of the 1990s.[13]

Any possible estimation about New Age books has to take the actual book market into consideration. Publishing books, more than ever, has become an industry. A book that won't sell will not be produced in the first place. A media society that hardly reads at all will, if anything, resort to the type of self-help and self-improvement books most easily, which, again, results in countless texts dealing with this sort of genre. Chandler also provides statistics for the booming esoteric book selling business: "Nationwide, at least 2,500 bookstores specialize in New Age books (twice the 1982 number); and 25,000 titles are in print, accounting for more than a billion dollars in sales in 1987 (up 30% over 1986), according to industry figures."[14] The overwhelming majority of white shaman books are, though almost never explicitly, a very integral part of those texts. In Part II, some esoteric factors of representative white shaman books have been compiled in a provisional synopsis.

The succeeding attempt to systematize white shaman writing employs typical New Agean features, projected onto Indianness as a hereditary version of classic noble savage images and characteristics. This New Agean Indianness is more or less subliminally confined to a purely metabolic function. The metabolism of Native American culture – as perceived by esoteric seekers – should restore the overcivilized body, mind, and spirit. Native American culture, thus, achieves a very submissive status: it is popularized by and through esotericism into a very pejorative Indianness, destined to counsel and remedy non-native customers. Accordingly, white shamanism is never so much centered on Native Americans and their culture, but on mobilizing esoteric Indianness for the purpose of finding oneself.

The tenor of Indian wisdom, Indian prophecies, and Indian vision quests is always and exclusively colored by customary New Agean features. Several of the most prominent of these features have been deciphered (and classified by six major categories) for Part II. All of these features, then, have been dissected and scrutinized with regard to their appropriation of typically esotericized Indianness. For this purpose, nine books by ten different authors have been selected to provide illustrative examples. The authors, all ten of them descending from Caucasian (i.e., U.S. American and British) as well as esoteric backgrounds, display a prototypical medley of obvious white shamanistic features in their writing. Expropriating New Agean Indianness, they cleave to an overall stereotypical interpretation of Native American culture. However, by teaching grandiloquent Indian ways to their esoteric readers, they consider themselves a spiritual intelligentsia of that culture. Consequently, they become more voluble than native writers in the eyes of those readers.

By transplanting the New Agean paroxysm of (instant) enlightenment onto Indianness, white shaman writers pontificate a formulaic, yet equivocal style of writing. All of their nine books exemplify this style of white shamanic writing for an explicitly esoteric Indian audience. Those white shamanic teachings mainly focus on a sequentially extant Indian life for the matter of (Caucasian) self-improvement. The aspect of self-improvement, however, is never sermonized as self-help in an 'I'm dysfunctional, you're dysfunctional' tradition,[15] since this would be too negative a connotation for New Agean taste. Rather, white shamans' trespassing on Indian grounds is amplified through a particular piquancy as well as a certain euphemistic/diplomatic 'Have a nice day' policy, which will never leave readers with a bitter taste in their mouths.

Furthermore, white shamans favor a very personalized style of writing. For instance, they tell their disciples stories about their penchant for their personal spirit animals, about adopting their Indian name, or about meeting their Indian trustees – mostly Plastic Medicine (Wo)Men providing them with victuals for their vision quests. Interestingly enough, white shamans, though sometimes tarnishing opponents (usually New Age skeptics or Native American critics, of course), never vie with Plastic Medicine (Wo)Men about esoteric customers. They appear like a big happy family – Plastic Medicine (Wo)Men mostly conducting Indian workshops, white shamans mostly lecturing about or writing Indian books – each group directing esoteric seekers also to the other. By not interfering or even rivaling with each others metier, white shamans and Plastic Medicine (Wo)Men, thus, ensure the optimum of esoteric recruits (i.e., readers *and* workshop seminar participants). Meting out each others territory, necessarily, is also an evaluation of blood versus mind factors, as discussed in the previous chapters. White shamans – 'Indianized' in mind/spirit – fulfill the 'intellectual' tasks like writing books and lecturing on them. Whereas they resemble the 'thinkers,' Plastic Medicine (Wo)Men, in comparison, are the 'doers,' pursuing outdoor activities like sweat hut seminars and vision quest jamborees. Since most Plastic Medicine (Wo)Men claim Indiannes by heritage, their business becomes easily detachable to white shamanism, asserting the blood-mind dyad.

As already stressed, white shaman assemblage of books has turned exuberant to a point of quantitative immensity. Vague estimations about books on (white) shamanism being disseminated worldwide include about 30,000 titles – numbers proliferating. For the research chapters of Part II, nine emblematic white shaman texts have been selected (authors' names in alphabetical order): *Teachings around the Scared Wheel: Finding the Soul of the Dreamtime* (1990) by Lynn V.

Andrews, *Animal-Speak: The Spiritual and Magical Powers of Creatures Great and Small* (1998) by Ted Andrews, *Spirit Stones* (1997) by Michael Bromley (a.k.a. Growling Bear) with Kate Swainson, *Healing Quest: In the Sacred Space of the Medicine Wheel* (1997) by Marie Herbert, *The Hopi Survival Kit* (1997) by Thomas E. Mails, *Medicine Wheel Ceremonies: Ancient Philosophies for Use in Modern Day Life* (1996) by Vicki May and Cindy V. Rodberg, *The Medicine Way: A Shamanic Path to Self Mastery* (1998) by Kenneth Meadows, *Shakti Woman: Feeling Our Fire, Healing Our World, The New Female Shamanism* (1991) by Vicki Noble, *Totems: The Transformative Power of Your Personal Animal Totem* (1997) by Brad Steiger.

In *Teachings around the Sacred Wheel: Finding the Soul of the Dreamtime*, Lynn V. Andrews promises readers that they "can participate directly in a vision quest for enlightenment and personal power."[16] What sounds like a mega-New Agean life show that "millions of Lynn Andrews's readers"[17] are privileged to witness, is a fine masterpiece of the esoteric game of 'taking no sides.' Andrews, a Los Angeles and Santa Fe resident – preferably wearing primitive jewelry (like, for example, Hopi 'fetish' necklaces) – also presents her *Teachings* as motley mixture of primitive wisdom, her favorite brainchild, still, being the Indian (woman shaman). Dedicating *Teachings* to her token informants "Agnes Whistling Elk" and "Ruby Plenty Chiefs," as well as to her self-made "Sisterhood of the Shields, and the Great Beings of the Dreamtime,"[18] Andrews keeps her background of Indian respondents as vague as possible, giving herself ample opportunity to shift in between (cultural) sides without clearly disclosing her sources. It is therefore that most of Andrews' critics claim that she 'can write almost anything and get away with it.'

Ted Andrews' *Animal-Speak: The Spiritual and Magical Powers of Creatures Great and Small* is a typical example of how New Agean interpretations of environmentalism intermingle with Indianness. Andrews is characterized as "a full-time author, student, and teacher in the metaphysical and spiritual fields," conducting "seminars, symposiums, workshops, and lectures on ancient mysticism, focusing on translating esoteric material to make it comprehensible and practical for everyone."[19] Accordingly, *Animal-Speak* is advertised as means to "reconnect with life's greatest teachers" – animals: "Animals will become a part of you, revealing to you the majesty and divine in all life. They will restore your childlike wonder of the world and strengthen your belief in magic, dreams and possibilities."[20] Thus, the main purpose of *Animal-Speak* is made quite clear: nature is not intended to be comprehended, but esotericized for the mere reason of New Agean self-fulfillment. Flavored and exoticized through New Agean Indianness, each environmental encounter, then, turns into a rite of passage for personal enlightenment.

Printed in Italy and written by a Celtic (i.e., British) shaman, Michael Bromley's *Spirit Stones* shows how cosmopolitan New Age Indianness can be. Besides, *Spirit Stones* is also a fine example of esoteric playfulness attached to the 'Indian way,' for Grandfather Michael's instruction book for instant happiness/enlightenment comes along with a set of twelve neat trinket stones and a so-called Sacred Spiral Cloth. His disciples, thus, can experiment with New Age Indianness like kids with their Christmas chemistry set. Bromley, though giving some basic instructions on the stones and the cloth, is very clear about the seekers' individual readings of the stones. This, of course, is a welcome warrant for working with the stones in any way that would ensure the desired result. Therefore, *Spirit Stones* is the prototypical, pocket-sized D-I-Y-book of customer-friendly Indian esotericism. The main principle is to keep esoteric seekers satisfied by guaranteeing a hundred percent success rate, with self-improvement and balance in life coming about flawlessly.

Marie Herbert's *Healing Quest: In the Sacred Space of the Medicine Wheel* gives a personal account of the author's healing crisis after the sudden death of her youngest daughter. What is told in the form of a half-year rite of passage through the U.S. Southwest, however, has not so much to do with coping with the loss of a child, but crystallizes into a vision quest of New Age Indian style. Herbert's midlife/identity crisis primarily deals with 'a path beyond motherhood' under the guidance of wise Indian teachers and peaks in her adopting an Indian name and assuming the role of an elderly (medicine) woman: "[L]aughter spills out of me every time I see or think of Sunlight Through The Trees."[21]

This outcome of the quest, naturally, corresponds with Herbert's traditional occupation as "transformational therapist."[22] Herbert, undoubtedly descending from a sworn New Age background, resorts to Indians as esoteric consultants to discover a particularly easy variant of enlightenment. By experiencing a commodious, smooth, workshop-like vision quest, maternally monitored and served by well-meaning Indians, Herbert is effortlessly empowered by (female) shamanism. *Healing Quest* develops into a pleading for listening to 'the Indian in all of us,' decorated with references to typically New Agean sources such as Fritjof Capra and "arcane wisdom."[23] Actually, it does not only represent New Agean Indianness, but also New Agean Indianness as a painkiller for alienated, overcivilized readers. Herbert is very explicit about each of her family members (i.e., her husband and her elder daughter) doing 'their own things.' Dealing with their crisis in life is not so much a family issue, except for their annual meditation around the globe. Herbert, the British citizen, rather makes herself appear as the individual, being adopted by her newly found 'Indian friends.' This shift to New Age Indianness as substitute (tribal) community makes *Healing Quest* especially attractive for single esoteric readers.

Thomas E. Mails is fervent to record Indian wisdom and mysticism for civilized posterity. Differentiating quite radically between 'good' Indians (those who co-operate with him) and 'bad' Indians (those who won't), Mails assumes the role of the interpreter of 'Indian ways,' unselfishly trying to enlighten his readers with *The Hopi Survival Kit*. Mails, who, of course, has been chosen by Indians themselves to become an expert in their ways, showers his readers with prophecies, instructions, and warnings:

> Think of it! What was missing here comprised nearly eleven years of personal and honest insights into the Traditionalist Hopi mind and teachings by five of the wisest Hopi leaders from Hotevilla. It is a treasury of information compiled by men whose life-long goal was to carry on a superb heritage.[24]

This expertise in New Age Indianness – one of Mails' ten other books "on Native American individuals and cultures," *Mystic Warriors of the Plains*, apparently "served as the primary sourcebook for the epic film, *Dances With Wolves*"[25] – is proved by a plethora of the obligatory 'authentic' photographic footage. This almost apocalyptic documentation of the Hopi as the spiritually prophetic/wise tribe (as compared to the 'selfish,' for secretive, Navajo, for example) is particularly significant for dispensing New Age Indianness to a clientele, who would not necessarily be interested in it otherwise. Mails basically recruits new esoteric Indians by, first of all, enhancing Indianness with mysticism, and, secondly, by making *The Survival Kit* look like a universal millennialist bible for anyone believing in and fearing a dawn of eschatological times.

The subtitle to Vicki May's and Cindy V. Rodberg's *Medicine Wheel Ceremonies* epitomizes the basic aim of the two authors very clearly: teaching *Ancient Philosophies for Use in Modern Day Life*. May and

Rodberg, both residents of Salt Lake City, who – according to their publisher *Naturegraph* – admire and love nature, emphasize their role as teachers of other 'two-legged,' alienated from their 'Relations.' Ho! – They do not only try to accomplish their aim by occasionally adopting this clear Tonto style, but also by utilizing New Agers' most favorite Indian tool: the Medicine Wheel. The cast, thus, stays the classic one. The Indian, the ancient, yet wise, is made to enlighten the overcivilized, modern citizen – everything, of course, supervised by May and Rodberg. Both authors, though sharing the same interests in archeology, anthropology, astronomy, and the "sincere desire to find the deeper meaning of life"[26] – usually favorably pursued by white shamans – stay explicitly modest by never referring to themselves as shamans. (This is just a hunch, but, living in Utah, they might be LDS, which might not go well with the term 'shaman' – despite the Mormons' general fascination with Indians as being supposedly one of 'The Ten Lost Tribes'). Instead, they are content with distributing the 'philosophy of the Medicine Wheel.' Since they advertise *The Wheel* as practical handbook with step-by-step instructions, aimed at modern readers to overcome obstacles in their lives, May/Rodberg do not shy away to sometimes use drastic similes, which are not free from a certain unintentional comic effect. For example, they consider it necessary to make the overcivilized, unimaginative two-legged enliven New Age Indianness through encumbered movie images. During instructions to visions in a meditative Group Journey Ceremony, for instance, they compare an imaginative "white light surrounding you" to "the Force in Star Wars," while the vision of a 'power animal' as spirit guide during a Guidance Ceremony could turn out as "rabbit that is six feet tall, like James Stewart's Harvey."[27]

In *The Medicine Way: A Shamanic Path to Self Mastery*, Kenneth Meadows, who "has pursued his interest in the esoteric knowledge of ancient peoples for many years,"[28] tries to convince his esoteric readers that they "were destined to pick up this book."[29] Meadows exploits a wide New Agean spectrum, ranging from chakras, auras, and reincarnation to shoptalk about 'The Great Serpent Mound' in Ohio, 'The Mayan Indian Crystal Skull,' and Atlantis. While praising *The Medicine Way* for a "lack of dogmatism,"[30] Meadows is eager to explain his (severely dogmatic) findings about Indian environmentalism. Further, his 'Noble Red Man,' living in harmony with 'Mother Earth,' seems to have one ambition only: the enlightenment of esoteric seekers.

Vicki Noble is somewhat the New Ager par excellence, making even white shamans like Lynn V. Andrews, for example, look like skeptics. Dedicating her *Shakti Woman: Feeling Our Fire, Healing Our World, The New Female Shamanism* to "the Dark Goddess, who has been rejected and demonized by patriarchal culture and lies dormant in all women,"[31] she tells her life story of esoteric enlightenment, peppered with esoteric fury and shamanic wisdom. In this autobiographic Bildungsroman, Noble describes herself as having assumed numerous roles in her life when it comes to ideologies, beliefs, and sexuality, ranging from feminist rights activist in the 1960s to mother in the 1970s to shaman, healer, teacher, artist in the 1980s, turning from straight to gay to bisexual. This kaleidoscope of roles and beliefs mirrors her collective stance towards indigenous cultures/peoples. *Shakti Woman* exemplifies Noble's New Agean appropriation of a variety of native people, strictly portrayed as prehistoric tribes, so that their mere function is to juxtapose civilization. Interestingly enough, her New Female Shamanism is merely evaluated through bits and pieces of primitivist 'evidence' that fits into her esoteric worldview. This technique, originally developed by Noble to back up her statements while ignoring facts that would contradict them, results in more or less entertaining stylistic excrescences. For example, Indian culture – certainly being her most favorite neo-primitivist back-up – is utilized as (esoteric) model for Noble's story about how she became aware of her shamanic powers. While the Indian way to "cry for a vision"[32] is only mentioned as a decorative means, Noble quickly reverts to her 'true' esoteric teacher, Alice Bailey, making Indians appear forlorn in white shaman bathos. Parallel to that, Noble does not explain how Indianness and 'Mother Earth' are consistent with her, keeping 'pet' snakes (the snake apparently being her guiding animal) and proudly showing off "photopsychic art" pictures of "her snake, Bacchus."[33] Noble's esoteric opportunism, abandoning and adopting matters in free style, is ultimately expressed in her acknowledgements, where she thanks her "beautiful machine [i.e., a MAC II and a laser printer] for such good work" while a year before that having "maintained that the computer was the body of the colonizing beast that had taken over the planet!"[34]

Brad Steiger, a flamboyant character in the New Agean scene since the 1950s, has recently discovered Indian neo-primitivism as another means to pursue esoteric enlightenment. His *Totems: The Transformative Power of Your Personal Animal Totem* presents him as natural born expert on New Agean Indianness, for – according to himself – his "eclectic cosmology had easily blended with the symbology of Native American Medicine Power."[35] Describing himself as having "always been fascinated by prehistory"[36] – and Indianness to Steiger, undoubtedly, is strictly bound to prehistory – he perceives himself as mediator between 'the two worlds' (i.e., ancient and modern). This status is prudently bolstered by Steiger's presentation of references, quotations, and 'scientific facts' – all of which coming from an ordained New Agean circle. The so-called Transformative Power of Steiger's *Totems* is promised mainly through instant enlightenment and the acquisition of a personal, 'special' aura by working with animal spirit helpers from 'The American Indian Zodiac.' *Totems*, further, is advertised to offer "each of us the tools we need to tap into the power of sacred animal totems by finding our personal symbol and experiencing its energy firsthand."[37] What those tools basically involve are a full-time engagement with animal totems and New Agean Indianness, infiltrated by suggestive techniques that make no esoteric seeker withstand the transformative power (of manipulation).

It has to be emphasized, that this list of white shaman books can only typify a rudimentary and tentative collection. The findings presented in the succeeding chapters, also, have to be considered as a temporary – and still quite imprecise – exegesis on the popular science level. Part II, thus, is supposed to provide a preliminary and episodic assessment of white shaman formulas to fossilize, estericize, and synthesize Indianness.

Notes

1. Marianna Torgovnick, *Primitive Passions: Men, Women, and the Quest for Ecstasy* (New York: Alfred A. Knopf, 1997), 172-73.

2. James R. Lewis, "Approaches to the Study of the New Age Movement," in *Perspectives on the New Age*, eds. James R. Lewis and J. Gordon Melton (Albany: State University of New York Press, 1992), 5-6.

3. Ibid., 10.

4. Henry Gordon, *Channeling into the New Age: The "Teachings" of Shirley MacLaine and Other Such Gurus* (Buffalo, NY: Prometheus Books, 1988), 23.

5. M. D. Faber, *New Age Thinking: A Psychoanalytic Critique* (Ottawa: University of Ottawa Press, 1996), 352-53; Faber's emphasis.

6. Robert Ellwood, "How New Is the New Age?" in *Perspectives on the New Age*, eds. James R. Lewis and J. Gordon Melton (Albany: State University of New York Press, 1992), 59-67.

7. Kay Alexander, "Roots of the New Age," in ibid., 30-47.

8. David J. Hess, *Science in the New Age: The Paranormal, Its Defenders and Debunkers, and American Culture* (Madison and London: University of Wisconsin Press, 1993), 3.

9. Michael York, *The Emerging Network: A Sociology of the New Age and Neo-Pagan Movements* (Lanham, MD, and London: Rowman and Littlefield Publishers, 1995), 164.

10. Henry Gordon, *Channeling into the New Age: The "Teachings" of Shirley MacLaine and Other Such Gurus* (Buffalo, NY: Prometheus Books, 1988), 39.

11. David J. Hess, *Science in the New Age: The Paranormal, Its Defenders and Debunkers, and American Culture* (Madison and London: University of Wisconsin Press, 1993), 14.

12. Russell Chandler, *Understanding the New Age* (Dallas and London: Word Publishing, 1988), 131.

13. Cf. ibid., chap. 15.

14. Ibid., 133.

15. Cf. Wendy Kaminer, *I'm Dysfunctional, You're Dysfunctional: The Recovery Movement and Other Self-Help Fashions* (New York: Vintage Books, 1993).

16. Lynn V. Andrews, *Teachings around the Sacred Wheel: Finding the Soul of the Dreamtime* (New York: HarperSanFrancisco, 1990), back cover (hereafter cited as *Teachings*).

17. Ibid., back cover.

18. Ibid., v.

19. Ted Andrews, *Animal-Speak: The Spiritual and Magical Powers of Creatures Great and Small* (St. Paul, MN: Llewellyn Publications, 1998), ii (hereafter cited as *Animal-Speak*).

20. Ibid., back cover.

21. Marie Herbert, *Healing Quest: In the Sacred Space of the Medicine Wheel* (York Beach, ME: Samuel Weiser, 1997), 191 (hereafter cited as *Healing Quest*).

22. Ibid., 201.

23. Ibid., 149.

24. Thomas E. Mails, *The Hopi Survival Kit* (New York and London: Penguin/Arkana, 1997), 20-21 (hereafter cited as *Hopi Survival Kit*).

25. Ibid., i.

26. Vicki May and Cindy V. Rodberg, *Medicine Wheel Ceremonies: Ancient Philosophies for Use in Modern Day Life* (Happy Camp, CA: Naturegraph Publishers, 1996), back cover (hereafter cited as *Medicine Wheel Ceremonies*).

27. Ibid., 26-27.

28. Kenneth Meadows, *The Medicine Way: A Shamanic Path to Self Mastery* (Boston: Element Books, 1998), iii (hereafter cited as *Medicine Way*).

29. Ibid., xiv.

30. Ibid., xix.

31. Vicki Noble, *Shakti Woman: Feeling Our Fire, Healing Our World, The New Female Shamanism* (New York: HarperSanFrancisco, 1991), v (hereafter cited as *Shakti Woman*).

32. Ibid., 78.

33. Ibid., 45.

34. Ibid., ix-x.

35. Brad Steiger, *Totems: The Transformative Power of Your Personal Animal Totem* (New York: HarperSanFrancisco, 1997), 59 (hereafter cited as *Totems*).

36. Ibid., 59.

37. Ibid., back cover.

Part II

3. No Pain – The Instant Enlightenment Factor

A very prominent assertion of New Age spirituality is the scheme of 'enlightenment.' Everyday life is considered to be too unyielding and belligerent when it comes to deal with questions of 'mysteries revealing themselves.' Esotericism, thus, is perceived as counterfeit to this nonessential, for nonmysterious, life. Terms like 'enlightenment,' 'revelation' – even 'epiphany' – reciprocate in every standard esoteric stock of vocabulary. Principally, there can be deviated two irrefutable attributes of this certain enlightenment: it is instant and pleasant.

With these two attributes, esotericism responds promptly to the needs of its customers. The instant, spiritual help coheres with the fast-paced world by offering ready-made products of any kind. Customers' needs call for a quick solution to their spiritual dilemmas. Solutions, which should catapult them to immediate omniscience. Accordingly, any New Age product avoids dealing with a long-term continuum of self-improvement and, instead, promises tremendous change within short periods of time.

New Agers never protract the path to enlightenment any more than necessary by keeping it as simple and pleasant as possible. This path does not comprise painstaking efforts that would demotivate customers. New Agers are very creative in developing methods of castigating one's life as effortlessly and painlessly as possible. Enlightenment, most of all, should be 'fun' and free from any impression of hardship or rebuke. New Age critics discredit this particularly esoteric attitude towards fun. Further, they relate it to the equally criticized disrespect, New Agers have of anything that involves the slightest form of duty and responsibility. The pattern of avoiding or ignoring less agreeable aspects of life while merely 'pursuing one's own happiness,' is frequently authenticated as narcissism by New Age criticism.

New Age narcissism is very much intermingled with the esoteric faith in what has come to be known as 'positive and negative energies.' New Agers are very fond of classifying the world, its coincidences, and inhabitants in terms of 'positivity' or 'negativity.' Anything that involves pain, fear, death, war, hunger, and the like is labeled 'negative' and therefore categorically denigrated. This means that New Agers, generally, do not try to deal with problems in order to solve them. Instead, they attempt to blend them out of their perspective, since they do not want their lives to be affected by what they call 'negative energy.' This deviate form of 'sweeping things under the carpet' needs the dichotomous labels of 'negative' and 'positive.' Once certain difficult aspects or situations are conceptualized and abstracted as plain 'negative,' they can be put aside and ignored much more easily.

New Age fascination with instant, positive enlightenment has particularly escalated Indian hucksterism. Indianness is seen as momentous for gaining spiritual wisdom. The cumulatively stereotypical assumptions about neo-primitive Indian spirituality – highlighting entrancing meditation chants and adventurous vision quests – have presented it as the ideal target for esoteric seekers of epiphany. Indians are typified and adored as natural born wisdom-keepers, spiritual guides, prophets, and esoteric psychotherapists, holding the 'true' key to the path of revelation about New Agean mysteries.

In *Spirit Stones*, Michael Bromley promises a balanced life with the help of 'sacred animal stones.' Bromley's particular artifice is to postulate what can be called role models and case studies of instant enlightenment, that should convince readers about the power of these stones. He starts off by telling his personal story of how he became a modern shaman, how he found his shamanic path, and how he adopted the name Growling Bear, given by a Sioux Medicine Woman – herself apparently having no name – who would sense his "Bear energy."[1] By describing his personal step-by-step enlightenment, involving his worries and doubts, he demonstrates sincerity to readers, resulting in their trust as well as wish to become 'enlightened,' too. Growling Bear is also careful to not make himself appear as either huckster shaman or wannabe Indian. His shamanic path, therefore, can be read as follows:

> I consider myself a modern-day shaman; I practice a craft that is as valid today as when it first began. . . . Unlike most other shamans throughout the world, I have no shamanic lineage, no continuity of father-to-son teaching and understanding of spiritual teachings and ceremonies.
>
> I call myself a Celtic shaman because the Celts were a very old and spiritual people who lived over a vast area including England. I am English and want to keep my own identity; I do not wish to pretend to be Indian.[2]

Nevertheless, Grandfather Michael – as he is also called by his admirers – does not let any opportunity to appropriate Indian spirituality pass by unused. On the whole, native people or what they have to say are not really relevant: Bromley, the European, writes for an exclusively Caucasian clientele, who wants to overcome their hypercivilized fate. This path to wisdom and enlightenment, however, is not paved with obstacles. There is no stony ground, since the only stones encountered are the spirit stones, which should function as talismans. Except for a subtle warning at the beginning of the book to not fall victim to negative energies, customers are presented an absolutely safe and overall successful way of dealing with problems of any kind.

The *Spirit Stones'* attractiveness, most of all, derives from two important features: although there is some instructions about how to read and handle the stones, readers are provided with the liberty to interpret them as they please. Under the pretext of everybody's "instinctive side," readers are literally given a voucher for guaranteed enlightenment through the prototypical New Agean statement: "Whatever you decide is right."[3] The second attractive feature is the explicit integration of 'profane,' though tempting, issues like money, finances, and business. Having even set aside a subdivision for *business* – next to *health, relationships, journeys,* and *spirituality* – Bromley enables readers to pursue spiritual enlightenment, without having to resign from material wellbeing or having to worry about a guilty conscience about material wealth. He further demonstrates the effectiveness of his spirit stones for everyday life problems through five neatly – though not too obviously – constructed case studies: Rosie, the young mother, housewife, and part-time worker in her late twenties, struggling in her marriage; Sam, the business man in his late forties, suffering from a midlife crisis; Jennifer, the law-school student, who rather wants to become a medical doctor; David, the engineer in his thirties, who needs to reconcile family and job; and, finally, Miranda, the widow in her fifties, who is troubled by ill health and depression. Each of these probationers – the entire constellation not being free from a certain soap-operarian atmosphere – represents role models that readers can grab on to pretty easily. By identifying with certain aspects or situations of either Rosie's, Sam's, Jennifer's, David's, or Miranda's life, readers, first of all, bond, and, secondly, start believing that the spirit stones can bring tremendous change to their life, too. Thus, it is no surprise that each role model story results in a happy ending. Somehow, all five characters manage to overcome their individual obstacles in an almost effortless way, since they have believed in and consulted the spirit stones.

Healing Quest by Marie Herbert shows that a vision quest, elucidating one's life, can be achieved with the least efforts possible. Herbert's rite of passage (after the death of her second daughter Pascale) is not characterized by pain, hardship, or sorrow; instead, it is a pleasant (and entertaining) encounter of Indian spirituality in the American Southwest. What is specifically remarkable in *Healing Quest*, is Herbert's emphasis on 'pleasant,' 'easy' enlightenment. She is very eager to show that esoteric epiphany can happen to seekers without any detrimental distress. Her severance from husband and older daughter 'to find a new direction in her life,' is presented as an adventurous, but never dangerous powwow road trip along Indian reservations and from one Indian sweat lodge to the next. Her aim is to present an 'attractive' Indian vision quest done 'the Caucasian way,' the subtle message being that one does not have 'to suffer' to achieve a higher esoteric awareness.

In a very personal, intimate style, Herbert tells readers about herself, hesitating to endeavor on an Indian quest that would involve fasting in the wilderness. She heartily describes her doubts about going without food or drink for a couple of days in a solitary place. By expressing her wish for spiritual renewal while at the same time uttering her fears, she bonds with her (predominantly female) readership. As she also explains in the *Author's Note*, she considers her book as a guide in her readers' lives, as "a catalyst for their own journey toward wholeness."[4]

Accordingly, Herbert comes up with a lenient alternative to the traditionally strenuous vision quest. She presents a healing quest, specifically designed for women, that "was not primarily about deprivation, but about seeking insight for oneself and others."[5] This quest also forms the climax of her half year journey. Herbert tells her readers about spending three days in a comfortable tepee with a portable toilet, being waited on by Speaks The Truth and Looks Far Woman, two subservient Indians. She describes this purification process as contemplative time, practicing tai chi, recalling that "the universal truths are being spread" by Jamie Sams, Grandmother Twylah, Tibetan master Djwhal Khul, Yogananda – "a mystic and spiritual teacher from India" – as well as John Randolph Price and his book *The Angels within Us*.[6] This esoteric salad bowl poses no problem for Herbert, since for her "in Native American tradition, modern physics, and Eastern philosophy, everything is related, everything is connected, everything is a form of energy."[7]

Herbert's spiritual journey, bristling with terms like 'metamorphosis,' 'introspection,' and 'transmutation,' culminates in the euphoric vision of a buffalo, followed by an auspices-like appearance of five crows. Marie's return from this self-chosen esoteric solitude is eagerly awaited by a group of eight fellow (women) seekers, who congratulate her on the successfully conducted healing quest. The succeeding sweat lodge to her honor is a welcome opportunity to introduce herself as Sunlight Trough The Trees, her newly adopted Indian name, confirmed by the obligatory 'Ho!' This concluding sweat lodge ceremony brings forth a crucial aspect of Herbert's instant, pleasant enlightenment: the Indian as nurse to the white patient's overcivilization syndrome. The reason, enlightenment can be so smooth and undemanding, is due to the Indians' concern with the seeker's plight. Speaks The Truth, Looks Far Woman, and Walks Straight Woman seem to have no other drive in their lives but to provide spiritual therapeutics to seekers like Herbert. The neo-noble Indian, cast into the role of an esoteric nurse and caretaker, thus, becomes a mere inventory stock of the sweat lodge/tepee setting, handing epiphany to vision questers on a silver platter.

In their Group Journey Ceremony, advertised in *Medicine Wheel Ceremonies*, Vicki May and C. V. Rodberg promise an inspirational journey, 'unique to every participant.' Using evocative language, they describe a diverting meditative journey that finalizes the 'true' way in life. This true way, naturally, is shown by the vision of a neo-noble Indian shaman. Why this shaman wears one and the same "buffalo-horn hat, leggins, and moccasins" in every individual vision, leaping "out of the darkness"[8] and frightening all the participants equally – while each journey should be 'unique' – remains unanswered. The climax of this journey is the shaman enlightening each participant individually by telling them something *only they* can hear. This act of revelation is typically New Agean in its momentary character as well as its vagueness, which means that each esoteric seeker can come up with their own convenient truth. This truth, then, does not have to be justified, since it is 'individual' and 'secret.' Furthermore, the aspect of individuality – like the aspect of heroism, underlying this entire journey of epiphany – prompt the participants into harboring the memory of this 'rite of passage,' even if the rite itself turned out to be disappointing.

Brad Steiger's *Totems* offers convenient instructions towards expanding one's esoteric awareness through the help of Personal Animal Totems. This *Transformative Power*, as Steiger calls the way to epiphany in the subtitle to *Totems*, can be achieved easily and safely. All seekers have to do – so it is suggested – is to purchase *Totems* and to closely follow the instructions. Steiger himself provides a good example by telling the seekers 'his story.' The first chapter, *Our Animal Companions on Turtle Island*, presents him as expert on numerous New Agean issues, being particularly familiar with 'the Indian way.' He brings in several esoteric friends as well as Indian 'mentors' to state his credibility. This introduction, thus, does not merely serve to prove his expertise when it is meant to recommend and explain totems. Moreover, it is a way to establish his life story of Transformative Power as a role model for all readers. He also affirms this self-perception of being a teacher of and expert in esoteric Indianness by describing his adoptive name: "My adoptive name is Hat-yas-swas (He Who Testifies), and I was charged with continuing to seek out and to share universal truths."[9] – And Steiger has kept 'sharing' these 'universal truths' (particularly since the Indian boom started around 1990) through a book every other year.

In *Totems*, Steiger takes pains to demonstrate an itinerary to finding Personal Animal Totems, which would hoist the general wellbeing – with seekers being left to marvel about their newly gained hilarity. Steiger's assertive techniques to trigger seekers into finding 'their' totems are successfully camouflaged. His is a rich repertoire of simulated quests, relaxation processes, and vision quest exercises to 'enter shamanic time' or 'go on spirit journeys,' every technique subtly hinging upon animal totems. The basic intention is to make seekers constantly, though subconsciously, deal with animal totems, which will result in a 'successful' inspirational moment sooner or later. As every instruction is aimed at firmly implanting an archaic image of totems into the seekers' minds, the success rate of universal truth being revealed is preprogrammed. Especially, since "success" in every exercise "depends upon your willingness."[10] If readers do not find their "Essential Self,"[11] it is preponderantly due to their skepticism or negativity, but never Steiger's fault. Steiger, of course, also provides remedies for fighting this negativity. He even devotes two chapters (chapter eight, *Avoiding the Horrid Things of Darkness*; chapter nine, *The Healing Powers of Totems*) on diagnosing and curing negativity. He willingly shares his knowledge about negativity, stemming from his "analyses of over thirty years of conferences on 'evil spirits.'"[12]

Steiger's definition of negativity is prototypical for any New Ager. Situations or phases in everyday life, which might be slightly cataclysmic to esoteric positivity, are ultimately shunned. Then the mechanism of extricating oneself from an unpleasant or even conflicting moment is put readily into action. The motto for gaining a Transformative Power of the Self is to be blissfully happy: "When you are negative, depressed, angry, or jealous, you place yourself 'on target' for the chaotic, mindless, destructive vibration that comes from the dimension of the lesser energies, the lower frequencies."[13]

Notes

1. Michael Bromley a.k.a. Growling Bear, *Spirit Stones* with Kate Swainson (Boston: Journey Editions, 1997), 13 (hereafter cited as *Spirit Stones*).

2. Ibid., 22.

3. Ibid., 83.

4. Marie Herbert, *Healing Quest*, xi.

5. Ibid., 159.

6. Ibid., 165-71.

7. Ibid., 176.

8. Vicki May and C. V. Rodberg, *Medicine Wheel Ceremonies*, 26.

9. Brad Steiger, *Totems*, 9.

10. Ibid., 50.

11. Ibid., 50.

12. Ibid., 118.

13. Ibid., 119.

4. No Sides – On Neutral Ground

A crucial component of the recent successful rip-off of esoteric Indian culture is its implicit, yet consequent avoidance of critical, problematic, or controversial issues. The customer and future Indian-To-Be should not be bothered with profane aspects of everyday life, since it is exactly these they try to escape from. This attitude is steeped in a long tradition of both New Agean approaches to life (as discussed in the preceding chapter) as well as what could be called the 'socialization of ethnicity' over the last forty years in the United States. The sixties were a time of tremendous private and political interest in ethnic minorities and their cultural diversity. Legislative action was remarkable by the number of laws passed, which should contribute to the benefits of ethnic communities. This highly vivacious decade in terms of political action and alertness became watered down by a more inert political awareness in the 1970s and particularly the 1980s. Predilections of political solipsism vitiated socioethnic agendas dramatically.

Civil rights activism became more or less ostracized and the increasing political vacuum smoothed over by more idle ways to deal with a multicultural society. Deprecation of society as well as self-deprecation got facilitated through a wholesale adoption of cultural phenotypes such as the physically and spiritually statuesque Indian.

The 'gilded Indian lore' outlived any political, legislative, or social stance. Indianness – more than ever – became a commodity with no intrusive strings attached.

Also white shaman writing is particularly neutral when it comes to political, social, even religious, effigies. Its diplomatic mode aims at eliminating everything that would go beyond the preconstituted adamant Indianness. This Indianness is characterized by being retrogressively a-whatever: besides being a-realistic, it is a-political and – though adhering to spirituality – surprisingly a-religious.

White shamans are always very careful to never peddle information about contemporary Native American issues. They might describe their adventures on reservations and their encounters with 'true' Indians colorfully, however, unaffected by political or social predicaments. This, naturally, is an important delusive mechanism, which makes white shaman writing inviolate from any unpleasant handling of problems. White shamanic escapades on the reservation, for example, are always irreverent of actual reservation conditions. Never is there mentioned any of the quite diverse and profound difficulties most rez residents have to face: for instance, missing infrastructure, high rates of unemployment, drug addictions (particularly alcoholism), rape, infant mortality, and teenage suicide. Interestingly enough, diabetes clinics or casinos never catch the eye of white shamans. They never experience commodity food or any other of unique rez establishments, frequently described by Native American writers and well known to anyone who has ever visited a reservation. Instead, white shamans prompt readers into thinking that everything is not merely okay on the rez, but that reservations are areas of tranquility (particularly for escapists from 'the outer, material' world).

Another characteristic feature is the absence of any religious connotation in white shaman writing. Certainly, white shamans process spiritual issues, but at the same time they manage to vindicate these issues from any explicit religious context. This procedure is necessary for achieving a certain irreproachable outlook, which attracts acolytes from any congregation as well as outspoken atheists. Conspicuous New Age influences are equally mitigated, since any palpable resemblance with lineage from obscure circles would prove counterproductive with readership and sales figures alike. For the same reason, white shamans elicit steadfast denials of sect- or guru-like structures.

Lynn V. Andrews' *Teachings around the Sacred Wheel* is a particular variant of bringing in several angles of perspective. Dealing with a multitude of exotic features, customs, and rituals, Andrews tries to make her shamanic teachings as attractive as possible. Her overall concept is to serve her disciples as a spiritual guide/counselor, devoting "her time to writing, teaching, and lecturing."[1] This emphasis on the seeker's needs to not only get instantly, but also individually enlightened results in a plethora of tasks and cultures utilized. Uppermost aim is to win over esoteric readers by a number of ways, from which they can freely choose, and, of course, of which every single one is 'right.' The ones who are not entitled to choose, consequently, are 'tribal people.' Andrews, for example, has developed a clever strategy to circumvent indigenous claims, rights, or criticism: she invents her 'own' tribe – the Sisterhood of the Shields. This twist of realities enables her to deal with *all* indigenous sides, while at the same time being privileged to simply fade out sides that might prove harmful to her *Teachings around the Sacred Wheel*. As this title suggests, Indians (and the New Agean employment of the Medicine Wheel) are still Andrews' most favorite pets. However, she is eager to state that *Teachings* "is not devoted exclusively to traditional Native American tribal techniques; it incorporates the shamanistic teachings of the Sisterhood of the Shields."[2] Certainly, Andrews tells her readers about the Great Turtle, Scared Bear, Buffalo, and Eagle in typically Chief Seattlean style, and, naturally, she refers to her original teachers Agnes Whistling Elk and Ruby Plenty Chiefs, but these references do not amount to more than token Indian decorations. *Teachings around the Sacred Wheel* exemplifies uniquely New Agean flippancy of meandering in between. Andrews, considering herself as shaman within her tribe, has thus patented a way to safely wander to and fro (religious/social/cultural) sides and never give offense to any of her disciples.

Michael Bromley is particularly eager to pack his *Spirit Stones* with information about 'traditional Indian life.' He provides numerous pictures about Indian regalia and boosts his writing with stories about Indian myth and custom. Thereby, he manages to completely annihilate any implication that would go beyond a mere museum-affiliated representation of Indianness. The Indian stays the history showcase and the spiritual guide/prophet, with no chance for modernization or 'problematization.' If Grandfather Michael brings in problematic U.S.-Indian encounters in history, it is only to establish a certain setting for white guilt and/or the polarities of civilization versus primitivism. Exemplary for his deliberate avoidance of everyday, down-to-earth issues in contemporary Native American life and cultures is Bromley's *Native Americans and Europeans: An* [*sic*] *Historical Outline*, provided at the end of *Spirit Stones*.[3] This outline starts with the year 1528 and stops abruptly at 1900 with the statement: "There are only 237,000 Native Americans left, the smallest number since the European settlers landed on the continent."[4] The harsh break at the beginning of the 20th century, of course, has its reasons. It allows Bromley to not having to deal with anything that has happened to Native American life ever since. Whether it is Navajo code talkers during World War II, the occupation of Alcatraz, and N. Scott Momaday's Pulitzer Prize in the 1960s, or Native American tribes, filing and winning law suits over land claims – the 20th century and its political, cultural, and social changes as well as struggles for and by Native Americans are completely left out. Instead, Indians are frozen in history at the date 1900, at a time when they were sentenced the vanishing race. By emphasizing this picture and by not pointing out the recent growth of Native American population, Bromley supports exactly the stereotypical image of the doomed vanishing race. This stereotypical portrayal of Indians as historical, disappearing race, again, is beneficial for Bromley's *Spirit Stones* and its focus on ancient, neo-primitive wisdom for modern citizens.

Although Thomas E. Mails' *The Hopi Survival Kit* is placed in a highly spiritual context of Hopi prophecies and visions, he manages to neutralize any religious bias. Mails tries to strictly focus on the secrets of survival, based on Hopi myths and revelations. While he brings in apocalyptic scenarios, a set of commandments as well as sideswipes at the monopolistic stance, claimed by world religions, he never goes as far as to become openly religious in style or context. He is very careful to present *The Kit* as important, but not universal truth, free from dogma and, thus, applicable for and by anyone: "We do not want to undermine any religious groups. Hopi does not claim the key, for all people on Earth are responsible for holding the key to survival."[5]

Parallel to that, he advertises 'the secret' as amendment to traditional religious beliefs: "While the secret is not religious, it is nevertheless something that is essential to survival, for it is a supplement that every religion needs."[6] This strategy of not scaring away either believers or nonbelievers of any kind, makes *The Hopi Survival Kit* available to the broadest readership possible. By taking no sides, Mails tries to draft followers from *all* sides – atheists, agnostics, regular church goers, sect members – and, thus, enables them to safely integrate *The Kit* into their personal set of beliefs.

Notes

1. Lynn V. Andrews, *Teachings*, back cover.
2. Ibid., x.
3. Cf. Michael Bromley, *Spirit Stones*, 122-27.
4. Ibid., 127.
5. Thomas E. Mails, *Hopi Survival Kit*, 199.
6. Ibid., 27.

5. Being Chosen – The Elitist Group

As discussed in the previous chapter, white shamans are very meticulous to not attach any momentous, sect-like aspects to their work. Notwithstanding, they motivate their readers with similar methodological implications. The quintessence of these implications is always the same and surprisingly akin to common sect-affiliated rhetoric and/or strategies: a persuasive offer to 'become special' by being part of an elite group.[1]

The message of elevating one's life by being part of a 'chosen group,' still, proves to be quite veritable. Naturally, white shamans graft this message onto a very subtle context. The overall principle for this context is the notion of attaining special gifts by becoming enlightened. Throughout their books, white shamans would repeatedly rhapsodize about 'being gifted' through regaining a salubrious symbiosis of body, mind, and spirit. The promise of acquiring special gifts through how-to instructions, then, should do away with three basic obstacles in their readers' lives: the impression of living an uneventful life, the feeling of being unfit for life, and the wish to tether things in life.

At the same time, white shamans always include warnings about the danger of usurping such powers. They would caution about pernicious outcomes for readers and their environment if the instructions were not followed wholeheartedly and regularly. Informing readers about possible debacles in their ordeal to become a 'gifted one' is a double insurance on the white shamanic part. On the one hand, they can safely distance themselves and their writing from what they call 'black magick': by avoiding references to sorcery or witchcraft, they ban any negatively associated undertones. On the other hand – by sending out warnings – they claim irresponsibility if the readers should fail in 'becoming enlightened.' They sell this path to enlightenment as a blueprint, which the readers themselves are responsible to follow. The emphasis on clear-cut instructions and day-to-day exercises is a common strategy, which puts white shamans at liberty to blame the readers' inconsistency or half-heartedness for any unsuccessful results.

The aspect of the chosen, selected group also involves a certain level of seclusion when it is meant to consult so-called 'Indian experts.' New Age Indians tend to be a circle, closed off in terms of jargon and references. Quotes and bibliographies are limited to referring to New Age insiders only. Never is there mentioned any contemporary, credible Native American – be it poet or scholar. Instead, white shamans exclusively meander between New Agean sources – mainly proverbs or truisms of historic Indian 'chiefs' and Indian myths. Accordingly, any bibliography can be read as the Who-Is-Who of well-known New Agers. Above all, the restrictive focus on historic Indians reenforces the loincloth image, denying Native Americans any basic form of modern existence. The technique of wearing blinders to avoid contemporary Native American issues does not only cause irremediable damage to real-life portrayals of Native Americans, but it also inflicts a certain reversist nature upon white shaman writing. Not bothering with actual Native Americans, but seeking advice from fellow New Agers and peppering this advice with Indian stories and sayings of wisdom once in a while, makes authentic, contemporary Native Americans and what they have to say irrelevant to white shamanistic disciples.

Claiming Indian spirituality by extenuating actual Native American influence is also a crucial means to counteract criticism of what has generally become known as the Grey Owl Syndrome.[2] Being aware of the highly negative connotation of wannabe Indians, white shamans are very articulate in marketing a certain Indian life style with no need to obliterate whiteness.

Thomas E. Mails' *The Hopi Survival Kit* – more than any other book – centralizes the aspect of the chosen people. The chosen people in this case refers to the Hopi elders as well as to those white people, who believe in their prophecies and wisdom. Though never explicitly calling himself a shaman, Mails also presents himself as 'specially chosen' by these elders to distribute their 'message' to the white world. In the initial phase of *The Kit*, Mails is particularly concerned with explaining and justifying his work about *The Prophecies, Instructions, and Warnings Revealed by the Last Elders* – so the original subtitle on the front cover. Mails describes himself as getting to know these elders by mere chance, meaning that *they* sent him a letter, pleading to "Come and help us."[3] In a highly persuasive style, Mails tells readers about his doubts, worries, and surprise why particularly he should be approached by those wise people as mediator between ancient and modern worlds. He characterizes himself – descending "from an urban area"[4] – as being immediately impressed and overwhelmed by the Hopi land, "bathed in an aura of the sacred."[5] Mails goes on by expressing his gratitude to the Hopi elders for having him participate in their wisdom. By presenting himself as a believing individual, chosen from the masses, Mails offers himself as a protagonist, with whom esoteric readers can easily identify and bond. This, then, becomes the ideal starting position for his teachings of Hopi instructions for the future, consisting of commandments and warnings. By doing so, Mails assumes the part of the white patron, personifying the spokesperson for his Indian 'friends.' He even comes up with some sort of 'certificate of authenticity' with his informant's shaky signature and spelling errors on it, implying that this Indian would be by far too 'illiterate' to tell his story by himself.[6]

Outing himself as fan of Nostradamus' writings, Mails accustoms *The Kit* very much to this particular style of foretelling the future. His technique is simple and old, but still – so it seems – utterly effective with esoteric readers: he plays on common fears, drawing a worst case scenario of environmental, cultural, social, political apocalypse, while at the same time providing remedies for exactly those fears. Naturally, he promises 'one, true' way of survival, provided seekers will believe in the 'message' and, thus, also turn into 'chosen ones.' To explain his survival kit of ancient Hopi wisdom – the "revelations," of which he admits, "are so astounding" that he could not "blame anyone for doubting it"[7] – he does not even shy away to use modern (and very awkward) similes and metaphors. For instance, it is no paradox for Mails to compare prehistoric Hopi pictographs to computer facilities in order to make contemporary readers visualize the Hopis' traditional way of interpreting symbols to receive prophetic visions: "So Native Americans and other ancient civilizations who used symbols had their own computer system. The stone tablet of the Hopi is a laptop. The Road Plan is read like a stationary monitor."[8]

Vicki May and C. V. Rodberg approach the matter of elitism, when it comes to practicing esoteric Indianness, in a very discursive way. In an introductory chapter, called *The Malady of Our World*, they slander modern life that "generates unhappiness and discontent."[9] They establish a bleak and sinister scenario of 'isolation from Mother Earth,' of a 'bombardment from the media,' and of 'antisocial ways' of adults *and* children. What they then call "our collective failure,"[10] can be tapered by the sapient ways of the Medicine Wheel, which they, of course, are experts in. Accordingly, the succeeding chapter, *How We Can Heal Ourselves*, plays at the readers' wish to become a chosen one in handling this devastating overcivilization. Readers are promised to become empowered, and thus gifted by listening to "our spiritual side," they are further assured to manage the balance of "our material accomplishments with our spiritual capacity."[11] May's and Rodberg's instructions about the Medicine Wheel are praised as a remedy to not simply satiate the hunger for spirituality but for individuality as well. The Medicine Wheel turns into an expedient to become 'special,' guiding "you on your own sacred path."[12]

Brad Steiger's *Totems* is an ideal example to show how secluded the circle of New Agers can be when it comes to references and quotations. Steiger, explaining the Transformative Power of Personal Animal Totems by utilizing an esoteric concept of Indianness, does not ever consider it necessary to consult Native Americans beyond Plastic Medicine (Wo)Men and/or historic Indians. – And even those Indians are referred to scarcely. Instead, he overwhelmingly derives his Indian expertise from New Agean philosophers. Though certainly intending his *Totems* to reach a large, heterogeneous audience, ranging from seekers for self-improvement to amateur anthropologists, Steiger never leaves his esoteric background, when it is meant to back up his statements by predominantly New Agean affiliated colleagues. Praise for *Totems*, for instance, comes from Frank C. Tribbe and Raymond Buckland, each of these authors writing about 'metaphysics, the occult, and the supernatural' themselves. Steiger certainly does digress to Indians, but by doing so he filters out three absolutistic groups: the traditionals, the Plastic Medicine (Wo)Men, and the historic/mythic figures. Comparable to Thomas E. Mails, Steiger is very much in favor of the so-called traditional Indians, setting an example of the 'Old Ways,' so that wannabes can imitate them. Modern (and realistic) natives are abhorred by this esoteric circle, since they do not juxtapose overcivilization in a formally patterned way.

Like so many others, for example, Marie Herbert and Michael Bromley, Steiger, too, is very fond of (the enigmatic) Grandmother Twylah and her wisdom, repeatedly taught to white seekers. Paraphrasing Grandmother Twylah, Steiger concludes that "the traditional Native American sees the work of the Great Mystery in every expression of life upon the Earth Mother."[13] Accordingly, *Totems* is also rich in hints at what critics would be tempted to call Plastic Medicine (Wo)Men. As some sort of customer service, Steiger even includes an address list of 'Indian spiritual counselors,' whom seekers can consult by appointment.[14] These 'counselors' are another chance for Steiger to express his Indian-by-heart life style. This means that his emphasis on pointing out the 'mixed heritage' of these Indians is particularly significant. Julia White, for example, is such a case – conducting "workshops in Native American Awareness . . . operating out of Long Beach, California."[15] According to Steiger, she is of German/Catawba descent.

This inclination towards half-bloods amongst New Agean Indians is no mere coincidence. So-called half-bloods, apparently, 'know both ways.' The actual message included in this sentence, however, deals with the likelihood of gaining Indian potentials – a fact, esoterics are much more interested in than 'knowing about the two ways.' These valiant half-bloods are dissected by esoteric Indianness in two ways. First of all, their case shows that there is Indian capacity in all seekers, since one never knows about a possible Indian 'ancestor,' and – even if there definitely is no ancestor – reincarnation could ensure a former Indian life. Secondly, by combining Indianness and whiteness in a 'harmonized' way, the half-blood model validates New Agean eclecticism in terms of appropriating cultural trinkets as well as going Indian in spirit.

Together with half-bloods and traditionalists, historic/mystic Indians form the group of noble Indians, opposing any other Native American, who would not put their culture at display for esoteric seekers. Equal to the animal totems, historic/mystic Indians' purpose is to enlighten those seekers. The narrative time for 'their stories' is strictly past tense such as, for example, the story about the Seneca and how "they became a mature people of wisdom"[16] or the myth about the notorious White Buffalo Woman, retold by a 'visualized shaman'/'spirit helper.'[17] What it comes down to in the end is that these ephemerally wise Indians are utilized in the same way as the personal animal totems: they can be called from a dusty corner whenever esotericism sees the necessity to "create a spiritual-psychological mechanism that will bring about great personal transformation and manifest an extended sphere of awareness in an ever-expanding reality construct."[18]

Notes

1. This attitude is very similar to the common set of beliefs of any sect-like group. While white shamans in general distance themselves repeatedly from sects, their teachings about personal salvation are affiliated to elitist concepts of sect gurus, promising rescue from apocalypse.

2. So-called Grey Owl was a huge Indian attraction in the 1930s, spellbinding his (Commonwealth) audience with his revisionist, peaceful life, which was characterized by an experiential love for nature. This Grey Owl figure, however, got unmasked as an Indian disguise for a certain Archie Belaney from Great Britain.

3. Thomas E. Mails, *Hopi Survival Kit*, 9.

4. Ibid., 16.

5. Ibid., 8.

6. Cf. ibid., 40.

7. Ibid., 35.

8. Ibid., 324.

9. Vicki May and C. V. Rodberg, *Medicine Wheel Ceremonies*, 5.

10. Ibid., 5.

11. Ibid., 7.

12. Ibid., 7.

13. Brad Steiger, *Totems*, 6.

14. Cf. ibid., 217-18.

15. Ibid., 29.

16. Ibid., 2.

17. Cf. ibid., 44-50.

18. Ibid., 4.

6. New Age Eclecticism – The 'Trinketized' Indian

The expropriation of multiple cultural trinkets is one of the grossest elements on New Age agendas. Generally, indigenous cultures are rigidly patented, irrespectively of context or circumstances. The basis for these cultural trademarks is the notoriously capricious nature of esotericism when it is meant to draw from different (cultural) sources. The process is always the same: several segments of a pool of (cultural, scientific, historical, political) ideas are extracted, rearranged, and transferred to New Agean conditions. Thereby, the effect of piracy is incontrovertible, for this process does not total anything beyond oversimplifying and copying cultural trinkets.

Above all, this plagiarism is also strongly flavored by the quite fickle nature of New Age eclecticism. This means that only certain aspects of uncivilized life are invigorated, while others are completely ignored. Blending out unwelcome aspects, of course, is a means to allocate the target culture(s) to the white world. The question whether these cultures turn out to become trivialized to compensate white needs is never consciously asked. The triviality of 'trinketizing' primitive cultures is particularly fortified through the so-called art collecting. Lynn V. Andrews, for example, calls herself an art collector, being particularly fond of Indian baskets. Thus, indigenous objects are developed into tools for vision-hungry seekers. This 'art,' then, becomes the spiritual accoutrements for esoteric seekers, which – similar to souvenirs – they can invest in and later exhibit in their living rooms.[1] New Agers are particularly fond of running errands into the 'Indian Land of Enchantment' and its spirituality. Feeling ill equipped for life by their Caucasian cultural background, they readily regroup Indian trinkets to be integrated into exactly this background. The indisputable outcome is a certain sham spirituality with a loose array of trinkets, that can be utilized permissively.

As demonstrated in the previous chapter, Native Americans are not really entitled to an independent voice. Without any doubt, white shamans are appreciative of contemporary Indian sources. However, this happens only through the forbearance of the good, helpful Indian informant, responsive to white spiritual and emotional needs. These friendly, hospitable Indians grow quickly into Thanksgiving Indians, reverberating well-known stereotypes. The result is a mandatory classification of good/noble Indians and bad/ignoble Indians.

This allocation of principally two categorical types of Indians allows white shamans to justify their criticism of Native Americans, who are incisive to New Age Indianness. Several Native American writers and critics have remarked on the acrimonious stance of white shamans, whenever the deeds of esoteric Indianness have been questioned. White shamans consider this as a personal affront to their empathy and sympathy with Indianness. Naturally, they abhor the fact that their seriousness or honesty in terms of Indian spirituality is deprecated. Most of the times, they react by incriminating these Native American critics as inept and irascible people, not 'willing to share their culture.' What shines through any of these accusations is the assumption that native peoples just *have* to make their cultural heritage available to the general public, no matter what.[2] It is an absolutistic assumption that casts the Indian into the role of the spiritual pet – and anyone unwilling to play that role is charged with spiritually hidebound selfishness.

Michael Bromley's *Spirit Stones* epitomizes Indian spirituality being 'trinketized.' His book – intended to *Use the Positive Energies of Native American Sacred Animal Spirit Stones to Balance Your Life* (thus the subtitle on the front cover) – comes along with twelve Spirit Stones and a so-called Sacred Spiral Cloth to cast the stones onto. Bromley praises the stones as being "imbued with the spiritual power of the animals they show" and encourages readers to "become familiar with the power that emanates from each one."[3] He then goes on to explain each individual 'talisman' in terms of *world mythology, relationships, health, business, journeys,* and *spirituality,* also giving detailed instructions for 'reading the stones' by casting them on the Sacred Spiral Cloth. On over seventy pages, Bromley demonstrates eloquently and assertively how these 'talismans' can turn into a spiritual source for help and guidance in *any* situation, at *any* time, for *anybody.* – Or in his own words: "In life we sometimes need help to understand the energies that are around us. We sometimes find it difficult to decide how to tackle a particular problem or to see clearly what is best for us. Using the Spirit Stones will empower you and give you direction."[4]

These magic stones, actually, are very obvious merchandizing products. At a closer look, they do not even turn out to be real stones, but some sort of plastic stone replica. These synthetic stones seem to be fabricated in a way that their shapes correspond with the forms of the spirit animals printed on them (i.e., round stones for spider and frog; elliptic stones for whale and dolphin). Like the Sacred Cloth, these 'talismans' are plain assembly line work. How such knick-knacks, manufactured in mass production and purchased in a shop, can be enhanced with any form of spiritual power or should have the potential to turn into personal objects, Grandfather Michael never explains.

Bromley's *Spirit Stones* is also a good example of how decorative quotes by and references to very famous pet Indians can be. Bromley tries to promote his book by bringing in statements and truisms of Indian 'chiefs' and 'prophets,' particularly eligible in New Age circles. Frequent hints at Black Elk, Raining Bird, or White Buffalo Woman should legitimize Grandfather Michael's interpretation of Indian spirituality. This utilization of Indian figures for mere decorative quotes makes them appear as ancient oddments, no longer necessary for anything but adorn New Age writing. Equally diminutive are the name- and faceless Indians Bromley brings in to also ornament and back up his esoteric findings about Indian spirituality. There are mentioned a Hopi and a Yakima Indian, for example, who have no other task but distribute commonplace Indian proverbs. Being deprived of any context or identity, they are not entitled to become more than mere unfathomable figures. They are the good, but stolid Indians, who have the white man explain their culture. It even appears as if Bromley himself falls prey to his self-defined pattern of good and bad Indians by including William Leigh's (1866-1955) painting of the *Navajo Fire Dance,* describing it as being "characterized by vibrant styles of dancing."[5] Whereas Bromley cherishes this painting as catching the atmosphere of 'true' Indian lore, it is otherwise criticized as clear-cut white perception of brutish Indian savagism. Grandfather Michael's appropriation of this painting is exemplary for his general style of consulting predominantly white sources about Indianness. If anything, he excerpts prototypical pet Indian references and remodels them to divert his own writing.

Marie Herbert's *Healing Quest* is characteristic for presenting merely nice, friendly Indians. The introductory part of *Healing Quest* establishes Indians as spiritual counterparts to sober, rational white citizens, which makes them the ideal counselors on Herbert's planned 'rite of passage.' Herbert attempts a balancing act between providing realistic information about contemporary Native American life – to make her writing more credible – and diplomatically subverting information about issues that would disrupt her writing and disorient her readers. For instance, she only involves U.S. American history or politics as intercession to prove her concern with and deep respect for Indian culture. Most of the times, it is a mere alibi to cast Indians into well-established roles such as the exotic wisdom-keepers or the prehistoric environmentalists.

Every encounter with reservation life is limited to a minimum handling of day-to-day issues. Irritating the readership with problems, which might not be as easily solved as the question of spiritual enlightenment, is strictly avoided. Any of Herbert's efforts to convey the impression of political correctness, somehow, seems to be out of place. Like, for example, her apology at the beginning of the book for any possible, unintentional misrepresentation of Indian culture as well as the highly constructed dialogue with her daughter Kari about Indian cliches. Whereas her apology does not include a reasonable explanation why she, as a British woman, would even want to represent Indians (could it be that in her eyes they are not capable of doing this properly themselves?) the dialogue with Kari serves as a mere forum for spreading 'expertise' about Indian history, with Kari assuming the part of the ignorant white, unaware of the 'Indian side' (represented by, guess, whom?) By lamenting over Indian sacrifice, Herbert lapses into white guilt, which leaves room for two Indian figures only: the Indian victim and the noble Indian. Both figures are thoroughly exploited by referring to historic as well as contemporary Indians. Chief Seattle and an extensively quoted passage from 'his' speech (which apparently Herbert knows by heart)[6] as well as the

Cherokees and their Trail of Tears are brought in to establish the Indian environmentalist, caring for 'Mother Nature':

> Dispersed and relocated, mainly by pressure from white colonists, their Native soil was carved up and appropriated by the white invaders. Their grief was compounded by the fact that they shared a special relationship with the earth which they regarded as their mother. Every inch of it was sacred and needed to be treated with respect. To have the land torn from them was as injurious to their well-being as if they had had the heart torn out of them.[7]

Contemporary Indians are always noble Thanksgiving Indians, who do not only willingly share their culture, but who consider it even a 'duty' to enlighten white seekers, as Joseph Rael – "also known as Beautiful Painted Arrow"[8] – explains to Marie. Almost *all* Indians, whom Marie gets to meet during her rite of passage are – apart from some no-good, for too traditionalist, full bloods and Navajos – not simply friendly, but *tremendously* friendly, treating her as an instant "soulmate."[9] They share their homes and culture with Marie in a way even most believing readers will start to question. Though Herbert is somewhat surprised by the friendliness of her hosts, she fails to explain why anyone – Native American or not – should be so naively unsuspicious of complete strangers, especially when Herbert herself is "warned severely" by Kari to not "pick up hitchhikers, even if they're women," and to not "sleep in the car."[10]

As already evident in the title, Thomas E. Mails' *The Hopi Survival Kit* portrays the tribe of the Hopi – and particularly their elders – as wisdom-keepers and prophets for the Caucasian world. Focusing on Hopi culture for esoteric purposes is nothing unusual. In fact, in recent years, Hopi peoples have been increasingly stigmatized as deeply mysterious tribe by a vast number of esoteric seekers. Their ceremonies, some still hidden from outsiders' eyes, their Kachina Dolls, eagerly bargained for by white 'collectors' and mostly mistaken for some voodoo-like puppets, plus the area they live in, which has always been a favorite destination for pilgrimages of UFO worshippers, turns them into ideal targets for any New Agean projection of mysticism.

The first chapters of *The Kit* are significant for playing on those well-known myths about the Hopi tribe. Mails literally calls them "outsiders living in a world beset with turmoil,"[11] and, thus, casts them into the role of the spiritual, (but) primitive people, who store cures for the modern world. By building up a visible distinction between the civilized Caucasian world and the traditional Hopi world, Mails' verbosity limits the Hopis to merely this role. It becomes clear, that Mails is only interested in what he calls the *Last Elders* in the subtitle to *The Kit*. Also dedicating *The Kit* to "all of the Traditionalists who for nearly a thousand years preserved the message from the Creator that will enable the planet and us to survive,"[12] Mails affirms his interest in and compassion for the elders (i.e., the traditionalists) only. For him, they represent the noble Indians, living to the ancient rhythm of nature: "By following the instructions, the Elderly Elders as a group have lived long and productive lives, and they have been blessed with wisdom, identity, security, satisfaction, and fulfillment. As a whole, these attributes have given them an inner peace that is rare among human beings."[13]

Thus blessed with wisdom, those Hopis oppose what Mails contemptuously calls the *Progressive Hopi* or *progressivists*. Mails' strict black-and-white pattern leaves room for these two species of Hopis only: the traditionalists and the progressivists. By favoring traditionalists, Mails – at first glance – takes a somewhat different course than other white seekers. Usually, white seekers would always resort to what they refer to as half-bloods (i.e., less traditional Indians) for esoteric wisdom, since full-blood traditionalists would never be available or want to be available as 'informants.' Mails has to slightly twist this common situation, because, in his case, it is the progressivists, who would not want to 'share' their culture. The basic pattern, however, still remains the same: Indians unwilling to resemble the peaceful, hospitable advisor for white needs are doomed to become the ignoble ones. The reason Mails inveighs against Hopi progressivists is their attempts to preserve some customs from the curiosity of white onlookers. This, of course, does not fit into Mails' esoteric concept of participating in everything for the sake of self-fulfillment. He takes 'Keep Out' signs as a personal offence and openly complains about Progressive Hopi not disclosing their culture. It is such passages that give away New Agean perception of Indians as either 'house slaves' or 'field slaves' (the house Indians also being ridiculed as '*Uncle Tom*ahawks' in Native American circles), serving upon white seekers of wisdom. Mails' pivotal intention is to exhibit Indians as prophetic, wise puppets; any native, who dares to claim some cultural privacy or refuses to look 'primeval,' is labeled hostile and inauthentic.

Vicki May's and C. V. Rodberg's *Medicine Wheel Ceremonies* is abundant with intercultural references to wheel-like, circle-like objects.

They try to prove the universality of the circle by hinting at bits and pieces like the Yin and Yang symbol, for example. This, of course, serves several purposes: first of all, it is a convenient introduction to their actual instructions about the Indian Medicine Wheel, secondly, it conveys the impression of their 'anthropological expertise,' and, above all, it legitimizes their appropriation of the Indian Medicine Wheel as a means to overcome what they call *The Malady of Our World*.[14] This appropriation particularly 'trinketizes' the Medicine Wheel by dissecting it for esoteric intentions to confront western materialism. May and Rodberg show a geometrically abstracted wheel that has been split up into two dozens fragments, each of them dealing with notorious New Agean catch phrases like, for instance, *mother earth environmentalism*, *female energy/shamanism*, and numerous *spirit beings*. In 0-24 steps and Medicine Cards (neatly attached to the book in a zip-lock bag), the two authors provide precise instructions about the correct use of 'their' Medicine Wheel.[15] What the entire process aims at is patenting this 'Indian trinket.' The Indian Medicine Wheel as patent for New Agean self-help, then, becomes distanced from actual Native American culture. The upshot is a trinket, which is entirely embedded into a New Agean context, suspending its original Native American reminiscences and, thus, any Native American claim to it.

Notes

1. Whereas former times have even seen grave robbery as one form of art collecting, nowadays, the proprietorship of primitive trinkets has become a predominantly legal issue.
For a discussion of the trend of auctioning off primitive art, see Phyllis Mauch Messenger, ed., *The Ethics of Collecting: Whose Culture? Cultural Property: Whose Property?* (Albuquerque: University of New Mexico Press, 1989).
2. As witnessed in a course on Native American Studies at a U.S. university, where a Caucasian lady would openly complain about two Native American students, who refused to 'show' some of their tribal dances.
3. Michael Bromley, *Spirit Stones*, 31.
4. Ibid., 80.
5. Ibid., 25.
6. The controversy over Chief Seattle's Speech, particularly when it comes to its authenticity, is discussed in the succeeding chapter.
7. Marie Herbert, *Healing Quest*, 11.
8. Ibid., 149.
9. Ibid., 45.

10. Ibid., 35.
11. Thomas E. Mails, *Hopi Survival Kit*, 1.
12. Ibid., v.
13. Ibid., 222-23.
14. Vicki May and C. V. Rodberg, *Medicine Wheel Ceremonies*, 5-7.
15. Ibid., 11-19.

7. New Age Environmentalism – The Red (Wo)Man Goes Green

A certain form of laissez-faire environmentalism is commonly popularized in New Agean thoughts. Possible esoteric customers are particularly enticed by a figurative understanding of nature. This means, that nature becomes an entrancing commodity, which serves the mere purpose of esoteric atonement. Any New Age handling of environmental issues hardly goes beyond paying plain lip service to central ecological problems.

Esoterics basically restrict themselves to indict mankind for a vitriolic behavior towards nature while at the same time cold-shouldering any references to or assumptions about individual, day-to-day ecological consciousness. Nature as such becomes manufactured into an esoteric hobby. The result is a certain armchair environmentalism, evolving around personal needs. Nature is, once and foremost, defined as a means to negotiate personal afflictions.

Also white shamanism utilizes nature as an overall tool to reimburse overcivilization and reconstitute 'inner harmony.' The principle of perennial harmony/balance is particularly overemphasized. Nature is dispensed into neat portions, that help esoteric seekers confront the havoc of technology and civilization. Indian spirituality is considered to be the most beneficial expedient to minimize nature to these neat portions.

The image of the nature loving Indian, being *the* first environmentalist, comes a long way. Tagged on this Indian environmentalism is the 'Mother Earth' concept, particularly well expressed in the nowadays notoriously famous Chief Seattle Speech. Surprisingly, this speech, although proven as fake Indian text – originally composed by a Texan named Ted Perry – in a *New York Times* article in 1992, is still treated as authentic in esoteric circles. Several authors have commented on the idolization of Chief Seattle. In *Europe's Indians*, Christian F. Feest, for example, considers this speech "a product of American manifest-destiny thinking," which would explain "Seattle's recent adoption as a cult figure by several Christian churches and the World Wildlife Fund."[1]

The 'Mother Earth' concept itself became also vindicated as stumbling block. In *Mother Earth: An American Story*, Sam D. Gill attempts to very much unscientifically deconstruct this concept as Caucasian invention, alleged to be Indian, which, again, brought Gill under the crossfire of criticism of both native and non-native scholars.[2]

Ted Andrews' *Animal-Speak: The Spiritual and Magical Powers of Creatures Great and Small* exemplifies New Agean self-fulfillment through esoteric environmentalism and esoteric Indianness. Andrews, calling himself "a life-long student of mysticism,"[3] sees *Animal-Speak* as a tool for modern readers to reconnect themselves with their environment. Nature as well as 'natural' people (i.e., Indians) are chosen to serve civilization's need of and quest for mysticism, which makes Andrews' focus of perspective pretty clear: the right to existence for animals and Indians – both juxtaposing the modern world – merely derives from the purpose of enlightening esoteric seekers: "Mother Earth is where we have come to learn and to grow. It is where we learn to free ourself [*sic*] from our limitations. It is here that we begin our quest for the Grail of Life, which is the quest for our true essence and how to best manifest that essence within our life."[4]

Animal-Speak, naturally, is advertised to provide a successful guide towards finding this Holy Grail of life. Including *A Comprehensive Dictionary of Animal, Bird, and Reptile Symbolism*, thus the sub-subtitle, it should serve as a blueprint for readers to decipher nature for their individual needs. How readers should be able to find or rediscover a unique way to their true self by following predetermined patterns and instructions (that are basically the same for everybody else) remains left to be answered. Instead, nature is nicely classified and the classifications nicely decorated with references to Indian culture. What is presented as the highest goal for esoteric seekers – individuality – is totally ignored when it comes to depicting Indians. Ever so more, they are doomed to stay one-dimensional figures, placed along impressive, yet vanished cultures like, for instance, Pharaohnic Egypt or Ancient Greece.[5]

Animal-Speak demonstrates this merely decorative, symbolic connotation of Indianness particularly well. Indianness is simplified as a visual ornamentation of New Agean quests for environmental and instinctual awareness. This is also the subtle message of the *Animal-Speak* book cover, showing a (white) shaman with explicit Caucasian features, wearing Indian jewelry of New Agean style, enhanced by animal silhouettes of deer and predatory birds. This cover is the visualization of Andrews' New Agean approach to nature and Indians: it is pet-like animals and puppet-like Indians, both in sterile surroundings. Andrews' advice for readers to go to zoos to get 'to know' animals, for example, formalizes this fact very well.[6] The suggestion to 'understand' nature in an unnatural setting of cages and iron bars is a flagrant contradiction. Andrews, however, is not at all aware of this faux pas of placing original wildlife into an artificial showcase.

A similar showcase is also reserved for Indians, displaying them as wise environmentalists. At once, they are being denied full status of humanity by being leveled on animal standards, since they are described as knowing animal ways better than whites, and – as if this was not enough – they are also being disclaimed knowledge of their own culture. As conveyed through the *Animal-Speak* front cover and Andrews' instructions, anyone can safely go Indian by adopting New Agean environmentalism as life style. Natives by birth, thus, are stamped as endangered species, restricted to museum environments as their final living space – just like zoos are conveniently justified and excused by their supporters for being the last resort for otherwise extinct fauna.

Kenneth Meadows' *The Medicine Way* advertises enlightenment by developing a higher awareness of one's esoteric environment. This *Shamanic Path to Self-Mastery* – as promised in the subtitle – is realized through common images inherent to the nature-culture dichotomy. Meadows introduces his 'teachings' by establishing a distinct separation between overcivilized society and primitive (i.e., 'natural') ways of life. Published within the *Earth Quest Series* by Element Books, which "examines aspects of a life science that is in harmony with the Earth and shows how each person can attune themselves to nature,"[7] *The Medicine Way* truly is colored by New Agean environmentalism. For Meadows, Indians, once and foremost, personify the most perfect environmentalists:

> Perhaps no people have been more maligned, more misunderstood, more mistreated and misrepresented than the North American Indian. These once noble and courageous people have been despised, denigrated and defamed, and most of it unjustly. In comparison with today's city dweller, they certainly lived primitively – but they had a wisdom that enabled them to be in harmony with their environment and to have a respect for it.[8]

Calling *The Way* "a book for the Spiritual Adventurer by a Spiritual Explorer,"[9] Meadows – like so many others of his colleagues – chooses the Indian Medicine Wheel as ready made exit to the "labyrinth" and "open-air maze"[10] of life. Meadows tries to bond with his readers by describing the personal set backs, he had encountered until he became a shamanic counselor:

> It will not, however, be a journey without effort, but you can be assured of getting to the treasure if you are determined because the author himself has already tracked the route, persisting in spite of experiencing frustrations and disappointments, keeping on year after year through youth, into maturity and into the autumn of years until he found the centre where the treasure is.[11]

This 'treasure,' undoubtedly, he found in a kaleidoscope of what he calls 'hidden' teachings, stemming from 'ancient shamanic' roots all over the world, which Meadows claims to have "adapted to the needs and circumstances of modern times."[12] Indian culture, however, is by far his most favorite shamanic source when it is meant to provide "the answers to your hidden needs, those tremendous longings and deep desires that have been gnawing at your very soul."[13] This flamboyant style is kept up throughout *The Way* in order to fulfill Meadows' most urgent issues: a portrayal of Indian harmony with 'Mother Earth' for desperate white seekers as well as a by no means less important portrayal of Meadows himself as incredibly wise and capable shamanic expert on this harmony. While dealing with the shamanic path to esoteric/environmental enlightenment, Meadows recycles any Indian stereotype possible. Frequently, it is only talked about *the* American Indian – *the* Red Indian Race as a faceless mass – with life and culture frozen into past tense. There is no differentiation whatsoever, except for ignoble and noble savage. Meadows attempts to be politically correct by dismantling the ignoble savage stereotype with the only weapon he can think of: the noble savage stereotype. Thus, he manufactures his own vicious circle of getting deeper and deeper into equally damaging noble savage images, while at the same time trying to criticize and neutralize historical cliches of the beast-like savage. This vortex of deeply patterned pictures of Indian environmental wisdom is kept spinning to serve the overall context of white self-mastery.

The plethora of Meadows' shamanistic explanations and exercises – ranging from New Agean metasciences of crystals and chakras to spiritual rites and adventure tasks – limits Indians, and, moreover, *all* Indians, to one, and *merely* one, role: the loincloth environmentalist, assisting white seekers on their quests. Above all, Indians are not only attached with an environmentally sensitive, but also esoterically sensitive aura. Whether they like it or not, they are linked up with New Agean Schools of Thought. The involuntary symbiosis of New Agean Indianness and genuine native cultures proves to be counterproductive to Native American emancipation from any angle of perspective. On the one hand, esoteric insiders consider Indianness as mere means of self-mastery – one even starts to wonder whether indigenous cultures would have any right to exist if there was not this capacity for New Agean self-improvement. On the other hand, books like *The Way* contribute to the survival of stereotypes amongst esoterically otherwise unaffiliated people as well, since these books – propagating New Agean Indianness by being ever so present – by far outnumber and, thus, counteract Native American attempts of making their voices heard.

Notes

1. Christian F. Feest, "Europe's Indians," in *The Invented Indian: Cultural Fictions and Government Policies*, ed. James A. Clifton (New Brunswick, NJ, and London: Transaction Publishers, 1996), 317.

2. Cf. Sam D. Gill, *Mother Earth: An American Story* (Chicago and London: University of Chicago Press, 1991).

For a response in favor of Gill's work, see Arnold Krupat, *Ethnocriticism: Ethnography, History, Literature* (Berkeley, Los Angeles, and Oxford: University of California Press, 1992), 40-41.

For a negative review of *Mother Earth*, concerning particularly Gill's research techniques, see Vine Deloria Jr., "Comfortable Fictions and the

Struggle for Turf: An Essay Review of *The Invented Indian: Cultural Fictions and Government Policies*," in *Natives and Academics: Researching and Writing about American Indians*, ed. Devon A. Mihesuah (Lincoln and London: University of Nebraska Press, 1998), 75-78.

3. Ted Andrews, *Animal-Speak*, ix.
4. Ibid., 34.
5. Cf. ibid., 7.
6. Cf. ibid., 9.
7. Kenneth Meadows, *Medicine Way*, i.
8. Ibid., xv.
9. Ibid., xiv.
10. Ibid., xii.
11. Ibid., xiii.
12. Ibid., xv.
13. Ibid., xiv.

8. Female Shamanism – The Powerful Woman Shaman

One of the most successful branches of New Age Indianness to cash in on is *female shamanism*. Women are a particular target group for hefty esoteric paraphernalia of Indian spirituality. By and large, the New Age wave has always formulated a certain spellbinding levity to coax women into what is commonly referred to as 'rediscovering their womanhood' or 'entering the secret paths of womanhood.' Such illusive slogans are aimed at recruiting a female clientele, which is particularly susceptible to promises and products for reorganizing and amending one's life. This adjustment of life is offered to be achieved through exceptional, yet minimally exhaustive means. New Age womanism, thus, incorporates one of the most obtrusive subterfuges of esotericism: instant enlightenment (i.e., the immediate change of life for the better).

Female shamanism occupies a central niche in the general complex of white shamanism. It is sold off as a panacea for women to mend the self-perceived debris of their (modern) lives. Female shamans jump at any opportunity to charge modern, civilized existence for the – in their eyes – deleterious conditions of womanhood. As a further consequence, they regard themselves as spiritual helpers to *all* women, who wish to indemnify those unhealthy conditions.

Since civilization and technology are considered as devastatingly erratic, female shamans are fond of endorsing the wisdom of primitive women, foremost Indian medicine women. Although every single female shaman is always very careful to appear impeccable to possible criticism, coming from either side – ethnic as well as feminist – they, most of the times, fall prey to their opinionated beliefs. By applying an inflexible black-and-white pattern of modernist-primitivist dichotomies to any of their assumptions, their teachings cannot help but remain dogmatic.

Marie Herbert's *Healing Quest* is a fine example of New Agean Indianness focusing on women readers. In autobiographical style, Herbert tells her (female) readers that it is possible to overcome despondency in life by consulting Indian spiritual helpers. In fact, by referring to one of her Indian teachers, Grandmother Twylah, as well as the theme of reincarnation, Herbert suggests that every Caucasian (wo)man carries the potential to go Indian inside themselves: "[A]ll of you have been Native Americans, some in more than one lifetime."[1] Herbert then goes on about how particularly women can enter 'the path of spiritual growing and awareness' to cope with dreary times in their lives. She does this by choosing a very personal style of writing, describing her own Indian healing quest. This healing quest, especially designed for the needs of women by involving very moderate forms of fasting and solitude, helped her – so she tells us – to find a new direction and meaning in the second half of her life. Herbert starts off by presenting herself as a mother and wife, standing at a crossroad in her life after one of her daughters has had a lethal accident. She resorts to several Indian medicine people to help her go on a vision quest that would reveal new prospects to her. The following journey towards female shamanism, then, becomes colored by two aspects that make her story sound particularly tenable: concern and community. First of all, Marie Herbert expresses subtle warnings about Indian charlatans, conducting vision quests and/or sweat lodges that might be harmful to women's health and psyche. She reminds her readers to neither fall prey to 'unskilled' Indians, only desirous to make profits, nor to what she calls black magic, including witchcraft or sorcery: "My reason for coming to the States to do sacred ceremony with medicine people was because I found their form of spirituality beautiful and gentle. The negative form of spirituality, or black magic, was not something I wanted to get mixed up in."[2]

Herbert presents herself as credible author, writing about credible Indian teachers only, who deeply care for the wellbeing of their spiritual students. Thus, it is no surprise that she quickly finds her way to *the* expert on female shamanism, Jamie Sams, who – emotionally arguing against wannabe Indians – advises her to do a vision quest the 'right' way: "Three women have lost their lives in this area in the last year doing vision fasts. It is totally irresponsible to expect a woman of your age, without any preparation, to be able to do it. In fact, it is criminal. You should not be doing a vision quest at all, you should be doing a healing quest."[3]

The main purpose of this and many similar passages in *Healing Quest* is to show women the harmless, pleasant sides of female shamanism – the subtle message being that they can easily become spiritually empowered by "the holistic principles of the Native American philosophy and tradition,"[4] without having to wear a loincloth for the rest of their lives. This aspect of concern about the readers expectations and wishes, naturally, is closely connected to the theme of community. Herbert, finding herself turned into a medicine woman at the end of her healing quest, presents her newly gained task as something special, yet achievable for anyone. Anyone, so she states over and over again, can experience what she has had – if they only pursue their spiritual journey sincerely. It is no miracle to become a chosen one, unless you do it 'right.' Thus, Herbert pictures her revelation of becoming a 'chosen one' in terms of female shamanism not as solitude, but communal experience, characterized by socializing and sharing in a sisterhood-like group of woman seekers. *Healing Quest* concludes with offering women readers an outlook beyond motherhood and housekeeping: the role of the wise, spiritually ever-growing woman healer. This outlook is based on an exceptionally esoteric interpretation of Indianness and Indian womanhood. Herbert's sisterhood, showing unmistakable similarities to Lynn V. Andrews' Sisterhood of the Shields, foregrounds esoteric self-realization, unheeded by any disturbing elements, which would come from either Native American lives or, specifically, Native American women's lives. Instead, Herbert offers women readers a model to grab on to when youth is gone and kids are grown. – It is becoming a grandmother 'the Indian way,' suggesting "that there is a wisdom, beyond that which we consciously acquire, which becomes available to women only in the later stages of their lives."[5]

Vicki Noble's *Shakti Woman*, like no other book, epitomizes the New Agean concept of *female shamanism*. With *Shakti Woman*, Noble, perceiving herself as shaman, artist, healer, and esoteric teacher, has managed to produce a fine example of esoteric women's studies, implying typical New Agean ways of eclecticism and dichotomizing about "The Feminine," which "is fragmented, shattered, and scattered about the earth."[6] Being absorbent of *any* primitive feature plus archeological or anthropological facts, Noble comes up with a radically constructed symbiosis of primitivism, shamanism, feminism, and esotericism: "This is the work I am calling female shamanism, a gradual mastery of oneself, and a healing or recovery from the chronic dis-ease of our time."[7]

This motley collage of 'isms' is bound to a frame of dichotomies. Noble introduces her findings about *The New Female Shamanism* (so the subtitle) by reiterating well-known dualisms. The commonly applied nature versus culture and feminine versus masculine patterns enable her to distribute ready-made answers. Noble elopes to an Elysian land of prehistory and matriarchy. These primitive/matriarchal ways, then, should oppose and malign civilization and its pernicious consequences for women. Thereby, Noble usurps the right to speak for *all* women likewise. Moreover, she regards herself as mouthpiece for native women, cherishing their ancient wisdom and feminine power. By telling her (female) readers her life story of a 'shamanic healing crisis,' she assumes the role of the mediator, deciphering the 'old ways' for a modern audience:

> Although I still live, like everyone else, in the so-called mundane world, I always know that there is more here than meets the eye. I have come to appreciate the little miracles of "synchronicity," or "meaningful coincidences" between the inner and outer worlds. They are the pathmarkers for the female shaman – subtle signs we can count on to show us the way.[8]

While this modern audience is supposed to be too ignorant to know about 'the old ways,' primitive people are limited to only knowing these old ways. Their rituals and customs are told in past tense and not by themselves, but shaman Vicki. Noble's tenure of aboriginal culture and its incipient but 'true' wisdom is particularly characterized by esoteric selectivity. The main (and mere) purpose of *Shakti Woman* is to stylize so-called 'feminine virtues' – intuition, emotion, and caring/nursing. And, Noble carries her concept of the *Shakti Woman* – 'feeling her fire while healing the world' – through regardless. This means, for example, that she only involves aspects, which serve the purpose of strengthening this concept. For instance, in chapter one, *The*

Female Blood Roots of Shamanism, Noble goes on and on about the 'sacrilege of menstruation.' She urges a woman solidarity of 'bleeding together' and graphically explains the universal powers of menstrual cycles. To verify this image of the physically liberated woman, empowered by menstruation or menopause, she frequently refers to prehistorical, indigenous (to her it seems the same) folks and their rituals.[9] As she also brings in Indian culture, one starts to wonder whether – since she is such an expert on anthropology – she has ever heard of the severe taboos, almost all Native American tribes attach to menstruating women. Interestingly enough, Noble never deals with menstruation huts, although these are commonly known intertribal features. Anything that would contradict her *Shakti Woman* motto of 'I bleed, therefore I am' in the slightest form is simply mitigated.

Parallel to that, Noble falls very much prey to cliched (patriarchal) predilections about feminine characteristics, while trying to portray the figure of a wild woman shaman: "Woman = body = earth."[10] By associating women in general and indigenous women in particular with images like 'earth' and 'instincts,' providing them with 'natural' abilities for healing and reconciliation, she involuntarily plays on stereotypical expectations. Her self-chosen dualisms of emotio-ratio/nurse-patient make her maneuver unconsciously into straight-laced gender patterns, undermining her statements about headstrong women prototypes. This fact, combined with the applied esoteric eclecticism, makes Noble's New Female Shamanism determined by a particularly manufactured 'truth' about contemporary women and contemporary native women alike:

> For Americans to let in the living play of the spirits, we are going to have to stretch our identities quite a lot more than those people living in other countries. This American phobia toward the supernatural, which permeates our culture on every level, makes the study and practice of female shamanism that much more complex and difficult, since women are traditionally understood as already closer to these taboo areas of spirits and magic.[11]

Notes

1. Marie Herbert, *Healing Quest*, 15.
2. Ibid., 40.
3. Ibid., 124.
4. Ibid., 119.

5. Ibid., 2.
6. Vicki Noble, *Shakti Woman*, 3.
7. Ibid., 5.
8. Ibid., 59.
9. Cf. ibid., chap. 1.
10. Ibid., 37.
11. Ibid., 64.

Epilogue

How does one encounter the past as an anteriority that continually introduces an otherness or alterity within the present?

Homi K. Bhabha, *DissemiNation: Time, Narrative, and the Margins of the Modern Nation*

The ontology of cultural multidimensionality needs to stay discoursive. Silhouettes of culture and ethnicity enthral most by being performative and never monochrome: a casino company manager, businessman first, Pequod second, a farmer family, counting Irish/Osage roots, and a single mother, who works as medical doctor and also happens to be part Yurok. – Native Americanisms, just like any other 'isms,' have been and always will be a multilayered collage of individual lives, beliefs, opinions. Yet, the phantom of Indianness might haunt the casino manager, the individual members of the farmer family, and the medical doctor more than occasionally. White cathexes with 'anything Indian' are incalculable.

When white shamans and their followers talk about their visions or color their lives as visionary autobiographies, they transcendentalize culture. Theirs is a vis-a-vis Indianness to Native Americanisms. The resulting reciprocity is somewhat warped and, therefore, diacritic. With white shamanism, Indianness is not necessarily highlighted as "*the product of a perspective*,"[1] but rather as a perspective in itself. By pontificating about the 'Indian perspective' in all of our lives, white shamans ventriloquize culture. Cultural Otherness becomes the product of this perspective and is further tailored to form a device for self-perceived preponderance.

Similarly, the white shamanistic, neo-primitivist renaissance of cliches about Indian nobility tendentiously relinquishes rights to as well as respect of ethnicity, while at the same time relishing the profanity of profits. White shamans' enfranchisement of patent medicine is decidedly flavored by consumer orientation towards well-to-dos. Sotto voce, white shamanism vouchsafes eternal happiness and balance for an upscale market. This is primarily, why sociopolitical signposts are not established within that market. White shamanic texterity of (Indian) argument never lashes out at affairs that would threaten consumer consensus. – Indian epigrams, more than anything else, demand what Edward W. Said has called "suprapolitical objectivity,"[2] for ethnic politics do not easily mix with an esoteric gumbo of self-help.

Singling out the Indian as the 'altruistic, demulcent Other' for Caucasian self-esteem and self-fulfillment condenses postimperialistic dilemmas. The erratum of Indianness as virtuoso memorandum of an ideal human existence or paradisiacal past is perceived by Native Americans not only as crying humbug, but also as dismal humiliation. The quite mendacious portrayals of New Age Indianness by white shamans cannot help but impel sarcastic Native American responses. Satire, perhaps, is the most adequate strategy to deconstruct and ridicule the paradox of going preternaturally native by becoming transitorily esoteric. Maybe, ironically, wannabe Indians – by overwhelmingly claiming Coyote as one of their 'totem spirits' – will mutate to clown rather than to trickster. And maybe – even in a more burlesque augury – white shamanism will be temporized by its own armament. Let's assume for the sake of argument that the 21st century will be the dawn of mankind colonizing and, thus, 'civilizing' space, with technology being the most important ordinance in realizing this aim. Wouldn't then progressivism haphazardly stop being a malefactor? With progressivism, again, condoned and rationalized as mankind's predominance, neo-primitivism, naturally, would be supplanted, banished, and insulated as ailment. Until then, however, New Age Indianness will interfere with some more impulses, unraveled by white shamanic erudition.

So far, the enticement of 21st century (white) shamanism hovers about (esoteric) writers and readers alike. Lynn V. Andrews, for instance, has already inaugurated the idea of the *21st century shaman*. – Going native commences immensely to signify 'going global.' The global market place has already been contrived for white shamanistic tribes, lifting the game of playing Indian in mind and spirit to worldwide dimensions. On the horizon of the 21st century, there originates the shadow of the neo-noble Indian as an international trademark of white shamanism. It remains to be seen whether this horizon will also offer ethnopolitical space beyond riding into the legendary sunset for an idiomatically vanishing race.

Notes

1. Jane Tompkins, "'Indians': Textualism, Morality, and the Problem of History," in *"Race," Writing, and Difference*, ed. Henry Louis Gates Jr. (Chicago and London: University of Chicago Press, 1986), 76; Tompkins' emphasis.
2. Edward W. Said, *Orientalism* (London and New York: Routledge, 1978; reprint with a new Afterword, London and New York: Penguin Books, 1995), 10.

Bibliography

Adorno, Theodor W. *Gesammelte Schriften: Soziologische Schriften II.* 20 vols. Edited by Rolf Tiedemann. Frankfurt am Main: Suhrkamp, 1997.

————."The Stars Down to Earth." Vol. 9/2. In *Gesammelte Schriften: Soziologische Schriften II.* 20 vols. Edited by Rolf Tiedemann, 7-120. Frankfurt am Main: Suhrkamp, 1997.

Alexander, Kay. "Roots of the New Age." In *Perspectives on the New Age*, edited by James R. Lewis and J. Gordon Melton, 30-47. Albany: State University of New York Press, 1992.

Alexie, Sherman. *Indian Killer.* New York: Warner Books, 1998.

Allen, Paula Gunn. Introduction to *Spider Woman's Granddaughters: Traditional Tales and Contemporary Writing by Native American Women*, edited by Paula Gunn Allen, 1-25. New York: Fawcett Columbine, 1990.

————. *Off the Reservation: Reflections on Boundary-Busting, Border-Crossing, Loose Canyons.* Boston: Beacon Press, 1998.

————, ed. *Spider Woman's Granddaughters: Traditional Tales and Contemporary Writing by Native American Women.* New York: Fawcett Columbine, 1990.

Andrews, Lynn V. *Teachings around the Sacred Wheel: Finding the Soul of the Dreamtime.* New York: HarperSanFrancisco, 1990.

Andrews, Ted. *Animal-Speak: The Spiritual and Magical Powers of Creatures Great and Small.* St Paul, MN: Llewellyn Publications, 1998.

Baird, Robert. "'Going Indian': *Dances with Wolves* (1990)." In *Hollywood's Indian: The Portrayal of the Native American in Film*, edited by Peter C. Rollins and John E. O'Connor, 153-69. Lexington: University Press of Kentucky, 1998.

Barkan, Elazar, and Ronald Bush, eds. *Prehistories of the Future: The Primitivist Project and the Culture of Modernism.* Stanford: Stanford University Press, 1995.

Barnett, Louise K. *The Ignoble Savage: American Literary Racism 1790-1890.* Westport, CT, and London: Greenwood Press, 1975.

Basil, Robert. "'A Vast Spiritual Kindergarten': Talking with Brad Steiger." In *Not Necessarily the New Age: Critical Essays,* edited by Robert Basil, 226-49. Buffalo, NY: Prometheus Books, 1988.

——, ed. *Not Necessarily the New Age: Critical Essays.* Buffalo, NY: Prometheus Books, 1988.

Bataille, Gretchen M., and Charles L. P. Silet, eds. *The Pretend Indians: Images of Native Americans in the Movies.* Ames: Iowa State University Press, 1980.

Baudet, Henri. *Paradise on Earth: Some Thoughts on European Images of Non-European Man.* Translated by Elizabeth Wentholt. N.p.: Royal Van Gorcum, 1959; New Haven and London: Yale University Press, 1965.

Bell, Daniel. *The Cultural Contradictions of Capitalism.* New York: Basic Books Publishers, 1978.

Benedict, Ruth. *Patterns of Culture.* Boston: Houghton Mifflin, 1989.

Berger, Peter L., Brigitte Berger, and Hansfried Kellner. *The Homeless Mind: Modernization and Consciousness.* New York: Random House, 1973.

Berkhofer, Robert F. Jr. Commentary to *Indian-White Relations: A Persistent Paradox,* edited by Jane F. Smith and Robert M. Kvasnicka, 79-86. Washington, D.C.: Howard University Press, 1976.

——. *The White Man's Indian: Images of the American Indian from Columbus to the Present.* New York: Vintage Books, 1979.

Bernheimer, Richard. *Wild Men in the Middle Ages: A Study in Art, Sentiment, and Demonology.* Cambridge, Mass.: Harvard University Press, 1952.

Bhabha, Homi K. "DissemiNation: Time, Narrative, and the Margins of the Modern Nation." In *Nation and Narration,* edited by Homi K. Bhabha, 291-322. London and New York: Routledge, 1990.

——. *The Location of Culture.* London and New York: Routledge, 1994.

——, ed. *Nation and Narration.* London and New York: Routledge, 1990.

Bird, S. Elizabeth. "Not My Fantasy: The Persistence of Indian Imagery in Dr. Quinn, Medicine Woman." In *Dressing in Feathers: The Construction of the Indian in American Popular Culture,* edited by S. Elizabeth Bird, 245-61. Boulder, CO, and Oxford: Westview Press, 1998.

——, ed. *Dressing in Feathers: The Construction of the Indian in American Popular Culture.* Boulder, CO, and Oxford: Westview Press, 1998.

Boas, George. *Primitivism and Related Ideas in the Middle Ages.* Baltimore and London: Johns Hopkins University Press, 1997.

Bordewich, Fergus M. *Killing the White Man's Indian: Reinventing Native Americans at the End of the Twentieth Century.* New York and London: Anchor Books, 1997.

Bromley, Michael a.k.a. Growling Bear. *Spirit Stones,* with Kate Swainson. Boston: Journey Editions, 1997.

Castro, Michael. *Interpreting the Indian: Twentieth-Century Poets and the Native American.* Albuquerque: University of New Mexico Press, 1983; Norman and London: University of Oklahoma Press, 1991.

Chandler, Russell. *Understanding the New Age.* Dallas and London: Word Publishing, 1988.

Cheyfitz, Eric. *The Poetics of Imperialism: Translation and Colonization from "The Tempest" to "Tarzan."* New York and Oxford: Oxford University Press, 1991.

Chiapelli, Fredi, ed. *First Images of America: The Impact of the New World on the Old.* Vol. 1. Berkeley, Los Angeles, and London: University of California Press, 1976.

Clecak, Peter. *America's Quest for the Ideal Self: Dissent and Fulfillment in the 60s and 70s.* New York and Oxford: Oxford University Press, 1983.

Clements, Forrest E. *Primitive Concepts of Disease.* Berkeley: n.p., 1932.

Clifton, James A., ed. *The Invented Indian: Cultural Fictions and Government Policies.* New Brunswick, NJ, and London: Transaction Publishers, 1996.

Cook-Lynn, Elizabeth. "American Indian Intellectualism and the New Indian Story." In *Natives and Academics: Researching and Writing about American Indians,* edited by Devon A. Mihesuah, 111-38. Lincoln and London: University of Nebraska Press, 1998.

Cro, Stelio. *The Noble Savage: Allegory of Freedom.* Waterloo, Ontario: Wilfrid Laurier University Press, 1990.

Deloria, Philip J. *Playing Indian.* New Haven and London: Yale University Press, 1998.

Deloria, Vine Jr. *God Is Red: A Native View of Religion.* Golden, CO: Fulcrum Publishing, 1993.

———. *Red Earth, White Lies: Native Americans and the Myth of Scientific Fact.* Golden, CO: Fulcrum Publishing, 1997.

———. "Comfortable Fictions and the Struggle for Turf: An Essay Review of *The Invented Indian: Cultural Fictions and Government Policies.*" In *Natives and Academics: Researching and Writing about American Indians,* edited by Devon A. Mihesuah, 65-83. Lincoln and London: University of Nebraska Press, 1998.

———, ed. *Frank Waters: Man and Mystic.* Athens: Swallow Press/Ohio University Press, 1993.

de Mille, Richard. "Validity Is Not Authenticity: Distinguishing Two Components of Truth." In *The Invented Indian: Cultural Fictions and Government Policies,* edited by James A. Clifton, 227-53. New Brunswick, NJ, and London: Transaction Publishers, 1996.

Diamond, Stanley, ed. *Culture in History: Essays in Honor of Paul Radin.* New York: Columbia University Press, 1960.

Dickstein, Morris. *Gates of Eden: American Culture in the Sixties.* Cambridge, Mass., and London: Harvard University Press, 1997.

Dilworth, Leah. *Imagining Indians in the Southwest: Persistent Visions of a Primitive Past.* Washington, D.C., and London: Smithsonian Institution Press, 1996.

Dippie, Brian W. *The Vanishing American: White Attitudes and U.S. Indian Policy*. Lawrence: University Press of Kansas, 1982.

Dorris, Michael. "'I' Isn't for Indian." In *Paper Trail: Essays*, 120-21.New York: HarperPerennial, 1994.

———. "Native American Literature in an Ethnohistorical Context." In *Paper Trail: Essays*, 232-54. New York: HarperPerennial, 1994.

———. *Paper Trail: Essays*. New York: HarperPerennial, 1994.

Dudley, Edward, and Maximillian E. Novak, eds. *The Wild Man within: An Image in Western Thought from the Renaissance to Romanticism*. London: University of Pittsburgh Press, 1972.

Eliade, Mircea. *Shamanism: Archaic Techniques of Ecstasy*. Translated by Willard R. Trask. Paris: Librairie Payot, 1951; Princeton: Princeton University Press, 1974.

———. *The Sacred and the Profane: The Nature of Religion*. Translated by Willard R. Trask. Hamburg: Rowohlt Verlag, 1957; San Diego, New York, and London: Harcourt Brace, 1987.

Ellwood, Robert. "How New Is the New Age?" In *Perspectives on the New Age*, edited by James R. Lewis and J. Gordon Melton, 59-67. Albany: State University of New York Press, 1992.

Ewers, John C. "The Static Images." In *The Pretend Indians: Images of Native Americans in the Movies*, edited by Gretchen M. Bataille and Charles L. P. Silet, 16-21. Ames: Iowa State University Press, 1980.

Faber, M. D. *New Age Thinking: A Psychoanalytic Critique*. Ottawa: University of Ottawa Press, 1996.

Fairchild, Hoxie Neale. *The Noble Savage: A Study in Romantic Naturalism*. New York: Russell and Russell, 1961.

Farb, Peter. *Man's Rise to Civilization As Shown by the Indians of North America from Primeval Times to the Coming of the Industrial State*. New York: E. P. Dutton, 1968.

Feest, Christian F. "Europe's Indians." In *The Invented Indian: Cultural Fictions and Government Policies*, edited by James A. Clifton, 331-32. New Brunswick, NJ, and London: Transaction Publishers, 1996.

———. "Pride and Prejudice: The Pocahontas Myth and the Pamunkey." In *The Invented Indian: Cultural Fictions and Government Policies*, edited by James A. Clifton, 49-61. New Brunswick, NJ, and London: Transaction Publishers, 1996.

Fiedler, Leslie A. *The Return of the Vanishing American*. New York: Stein and Day Publishers, 1968.

Fisher, Dexter, ed. *The Third Woman: Minority Women Writers of the United States*. Boston: Houghton Mifflin, 1980.

Gates, Henry Louis Jr., ed. *"Race," Writing, and Difference*. Chicago and London, University of Chicago Press, 1986.

Gibson, Arrell Morgan. *The Santa Fe and Taos Colonies: Age of the Muses, 1900-1942*. Norman: University of Oklahoma Press, 1983.

Gill, Sam D. *Mother Earth: An American Story*. Chicago and London: University of Chicago Press, 1991.

Goldstein, Kurt. "Concerning the Concept of 'Primitivity.'" In *Culture in History: Essays in Honor of Paul Radin*, edited by Stanley Diamond, 99-117. New York: Columbia University Press, 1960.

Goody, Jack. *The Domestication of the Savage Mind*. Cambridge, London, and New York: Cambridge University Press, 1977.

Gordon, Henry. *Channeling into the New Age: The "Teachings" of Shirley MacLaine and Other Such Gurus*. Buffalo, NY: Prometheus Books, 1988.

Griffiths, Alison. "Science and Spectacle: Native American Representation in Early Cinema." In *Dressing in Feathers: The Construction of the Indian in American Popular Culture*, edited by S. Elizabeth Bird, 79-95. Boulder, CO, and Oxford: Westview Press, 1998.

Herbert, Marie. *Healing Quest: In the Sacred Space of the Medicine Wheel*. York Beach, ME: Samuel Weiser, 1997.

Hess, David H. *Science in the New Age: The Paranormal, Its Defenders and Debunkers, and American Culture*. Madison and London: University of Wisconsin Press, 1993.

Hilger, Michael. *From Savage to Nobleman: Images of Native Americans in Film*. Lanham, MD, and London: Scarecrow Press, 1995.

Hobson, Geary. "The Rise of the White Shaman As A New Version of Cultural Imperialism." In *The Remembered Earth: An Anthology of Contemporary Native American Literature*, edited by Geary Hobson, 100-108. N.p.: Red Earth Press, 1979; Albuquerque: University of New Mexico Press, 1991.

———, ed. *The Remembered Earth: An Anthology of Contemporary Native American Literature*. N.p.: Red Earth Press, 1979; Albuquerque: University of New Mexico Press, 1991.

Honour, Hugh. *The European Vision of America*. Cleveland, Ohio: Cleveland Museum of Art, 1975.

Jojola, Theodore S. "Moo Mesa: Some Thoughts on Stereotypes and Image Appropriation." In *Dressing in Feathers: The Construction of the Indian in American Popular Culture*, edited by S. Elizabeth Bird, 263-79. Boulder, CO, and Oxford: Westview Press, 1998.

Kaminer, Wendy. *I'm Dysfunctional, You're Dysfunctional: The Recovery Movement and Other Self-Help Fashions*. New York: Vintage Books, 1993.

Kaufmann, Donald L. "The Indian As Media Hand-Me-Down." In *The Pretend Indians: Images of Native Americans in the Movies*, edited by Gretchen M. Bataille and Charles L. P. Silet, 22-34. Ames: Iowa State University Press, 1980.

Keen, Benjamin. *The Aztec Image in Western Thought*. New Brunswick, NJ: Rutgers University Press, 1971.

Kehoe, Alice. "Primal Gaia: Primitivists and Plastic Medicine Men." In *The Invented Indian: Cultural Fictions and Government Policies*, edited by James A. Clifton, 193-209. New Brunswick, NJ, and London: Transaction Publishers, 1996.

Keiser, Albert. *The Indian in American Literature*. New York: Oxford University Press, 1933.

Kolodny, Annette. *The Lay of the Land: Metaphor As Experience and History in American Life and Letters*. Chapel Hill: University of North Carolina Press, 1975.

Krupat, Arnold. "An Approach to Native American Texts." In *Critical Essays on Native American Literature*, edited by Andrew Wiget, 116-31. Boston: G. K. Hall, 1985.

————. *Ethnocriticism: Ethnography, History, Literature*. Berkeley, Los Angeles, and Oxford: University of California Press, 1992.

————. *The Turn to the Native: Studies in Criticism and Culture*. Lincoln and London: University of Nebraska Press, 1996.

Larson, Charles R. *American Indian Fiction*. Albuquerque: University of New Mexico Press, 1979.

Levin, Harry. *The Myth of the Golden Age in the Renaissance*. Bloomington and London: Indiana University Press, 1969.

Lewis, James R. "Approaches to the Study of the New Age Movement." In *Perspectives on the New Age*, edited by James R. Lewis and J. Gordon Melton, 1-12. Albany: State University of New York Press, 1992.

Lewis, James R., and J. Gordon Melton, eds. *Perspectives on the New Age*. Albany: State University of New York Press, 1992.

Lincoln, Kenneth. *Native American Renaissance*. Berkeley, Los Angeles, and London: University of California Press, 1983.

Lovejoy, Arthur O., and George Boas. *Primitivism and Related Ideas in Antiquity*. Baltimore and London: Johns Hopkins University Press, 1997.

Lubbers, Klaus. *Born for the Shade: Stereotypes of the Native American in United States Literature and the Visual Arts, 1776-1894*. Amsterdam and Atlanta: Rodopi, 1994.

Lutz, Hartmut. *"Indianer" und "Native Americans:" Zur sozial- und literarhistorischen Vermittlung eines Stereotyps*. Hildesheim, Zurich, and New York: Georg Olms Verlag, 1985.

Mails, Thomas E. *The Hopi Survival Kit*. New York and London: Penguin/Arkana, 1997.

Martin, Joel W. "'My Grandmother Was a Cherokee Princess': Representations of Indians in Southern History." In *Dressing in Feathers: The Construction of the Indian in American Popular Culture*, edited by S. Elizabeth Bird, 129-47. Boulder, CO, and Oxford: Westview Press, 1998.

Marx, Leo. *The Machine in the Garden: Technology and the Pastoral Ideal in America*. London, Oxford, and New York: Oxford University Press, 1974.

May, Vicki, and Cindy V. Rodberg. *Medicine Wheel Ceremonies: Ancient Philosophies for Use in Modern Day Life*. Happy Camp, CA: Naturegraph Publishers, 1996.

McGregor, Gaile. *The Noble Savage in the New World Garden: Notes towards a Syntactics of Place.* Bowling Green, Ohio: Bowling Green State University Popular Press, 1988.

Meadows, Kenneth. *The Medicine Way: A Shamanic Path to Self-Mastery.* Boston: Element Books, 1998.

Messenger, Phyllis Mauch, ed. *The Ethics of Collecting: Whose Culture? Cultural Property: Whose Property?* Albuquerque: University of New Mexico Press, 1989.

Mihesuah, Devon A. *American Indians: Stereotypes and Realities.* Atlanta and Regina: Clarity Press, 1998.

————, ed. *Natives and Academics: Researching and Writing about American Indians.* Lincoln and London: University of Nebraska Press, 1998.

Murray, David. *Modern Indians: Native Americans in the Twentieth Century;* BAAS Pamphlets in American Studies 8. Durham and Long Beach, CA: BAAS, 1982.

Nash, Roderick. *Wilderness and the American Mind.* 3rd ed. New Haven and London: Yale University Press, 1982.

Noble, Vicki. *Shakti Woman: Feeling Our Fire, Healing Our World, The New Female Shamanism.* New York: HarperSanFrancisco, 1991.

O'Connor, John E. "The White Man's Indian: An Institutional Approach." In *Hollywood's Indian: The Portrayal of the Native American in Film,* edited by Peter C. Rollins and John E. O'Connor, 27-38. Lexington: University Press of Kentucky, 1998.

Owens, Louis. *Other Destinies: Understanding the American Indian Novel.* Norman and London: University of Oklahoma Press, 1992.

Pearce, Roy Harvey. *Savagism and Civilization: A Study of the Indian and the American Mind.* Berkeley, Los Angeles, and London: University of California Press, 1988.

Perloff, Marjorie. "Tolerance and Taboo: *Modernist Primitives and Postmodern Pieties.*" In *Prehistories of the Future: The Primitivist Project and the Culture of Modernism,* edited by Elazar Barkan and Ronald Bush, 339-54. Stanford: Stanford University Press, 1995.

Pratt, Mary Louise. *Imperial Eyes: Travel Writing and Transculturation.* London and New York: Routledge, 1992.

Rollins, Peter C., and John E. O'Connor, eds. *Hollywood's Indian: The Portrayal of the Native American in Film.* Lexington: University Press of Kentucky, 1998.

Rosaldo, Renato. *Culture and Truth: The Remaking of Social Analysis.* Boston: Beacon Press, 1993.

Rose, Wendy. "For the White Poets Who Would Be Indian." In *The Third Woman: Minority Women Writers of the United States,* edited by Dexter Fisher, 86-87. Boston: Houghton Mifflin, 1980.

Said, Edward W. *Orientalism.* London and New York: Routledge, 1978. Reprint with a new Afterword, London and New York: Penguin Books, 1995.

98   *Going Native or Going Naive?*

Sanford, Charles L. *The Quest for Paradise: Europe and the American Moral Imagination.* Urbana: University of Illinois Press, 1961.

Scheckel, Susan. *The Insistence of the Indian: Race and Nationalism in Nineteenth-Century American Culture.* Princeton: Princeton University Press, 1998.

Silko, Leslie Marmon. "An Old-Time Indian Attack Conducted in Two Parts: Part One: Imitation 'Indian' Poems, Part Two: Gary Snyder's Turtle Island." In *The Remembered Earth: An Anthology of Contemporary Native American Literature,* edited by Geary Hobson, 211-16. N.p.: Red Earth Press, 1979; Albuquerque: University of New Mexico Press, 1991.

Simard, Jean-Jacques. "White Ghosts, Red Shadows: The Reduction of North American Natives." In *The Invented Indian: Cultural Fictions and Government Policies,* edited by James A. Clifton, 333-69. New Brunswick, NJ, and London: Transaction Publishers, 1996.

Slotkin, Richard. *Regeneration through Violence: The Mythology of the American Frontier, 1600-1860.* Middletown, CT: Wesleyan University Press, 1979.

———. *The Fatal Environment: The Myth of the Frontier in the Age of Industrialization 1800-1890.* New York: Atheneum, 1985.

Smith, Henry Nash. *Virgin Land: The American West As Symbol and Myth.* Cambridge, Mass., and London: Harvard University Press, 1982.

Smith, Jane F., and Robert M. Kvasnicka, eds. *Indian-White Relations: A Persistent Paradox.* Washington, D.C.: Howard University Press, 1976.

Stedman, Raymond William. *Shadows of the Indian: Stereotypes in American Culture.* Norman: University of Oklahoma Press, 1982.

Steiger, Brad. *Totems: The Transformative Power of Your Personal Animal Totem.* New York: HarperSanFrancisco, 1997.

Steiner, Christopher B. "Travel Engravings and the Construction of the Primitive." In *Prehistories of the Future: The Primitivist Project and the Culture of Modernism,* edited by Elazar Barkan and Ronald Bush, 202-25. Stanford: Stanford University Press, 1995.

Strong, Pauline Turner. "Playing Indian in the Nineties: *Pocahontas* and *The Indian in the Cupboard.*" In *Hollywood's Indian: The Portrayal of the Native American in Film,* edited by Peter C. Rollins and John E. O'Connor, 187-205. Lexington: University Press of Kentucky, 1998.

Sweet, Robert Burdette. *Writing towards Wisdom: The Writer As Shaman.* St, Louis, MO: Helios House, 1990.

Taylor, Annette M. "Cultural Heritage in Northern Exposure." In *Dressing in Feathers: The Construction of the Indian in American Popular Culture,* edited by S. Elizabeth Bird, 229-44. Boulder, CO, and Oxford: Westview Press, 1998.

Theweleit, Klaus. *Pocahontas in Wonderland: Shakespeare on Tour.* Vol. 1. Frankfurt am Main and Basel: Stroemfeld/Roter Stern, 1999.

Todorov, Tzvetan. *The Conquest of America: The Question of the Other.* Translated by Richard Howard. Paris: Editions du Seuil, 1982; New York: HarperPerennial, 1992.

Tompkins, Jane. "'Indians': Textualism, Morality, and the Problem of History." In *"Race," Writing, and Difference*, edited by Henry Louis Gates Jr., 59-77. Chicago and London: University of Chicago Press, 1986.

Torgovnick, Marianna. *Gone Primitive: Savage Intellects, Modern Lives.* Chicago and London: University of Chicago Press, 1990.

————. *Primitive Passions: Men, Women, and the Quest for Ecstasy.* New York: Alfred A. Knopf, 1997.

Turner, Frederick. *Beyond Geography: The Western Spirit against the Wilderness.* New York: Viking Press, 1980.

Van Lent, Peter. "'Her Beautiful Savage': The Current Sexual Image of the Native American Male." In *Dressing in Feathers: The Construction of the Indian in American Popular Culture*, edited by S. Elizabeth Bird, 211-27. Boulder, CO, and Oxford: Westview Press, 1998.

Vickers, Scott B. *Native American Identities: From Stereotype to Archetype in Art and Literature.* Albuquerque: University of New Mexico Press, 1998.

White, Hayden. "The Noble Savage: Theme As Fetish." In *First Images of America: The Impact of the New World on the Old.* Vol. 1, edited by Fredi Chiapelli, 121-35. Berkeley, Los Angeles, and London: University of California Press, 1976.

Wiget, Andrew, ed. *Critical Essays on Native American Literature.* Boston: G. K. Hall, 1985.

Williams, George H. *Wilderness and Paradise in Christian Thought: The Biblical Experience of the Desert in the History of Christianity and the Paradise Theme in the Theological Idea of the University.* New York: Harper and Brothers, 1962.

York, Michael. *The Emerging Network: A Sociology of the New Age and Neo-Pagan Movements.* Lanham, MD, and London: Rowman and Littlefield Publishers, 1995.

Zolla, Elémire. *The Writer and the Shaman: A Morphology of the American Indian.* Translated by Raymond Rosenthal. N.p.: Casa Editrice Valentino Bompiani, 1969; New York: Harcourt Brace Jovanovic, 1973.

Index